COMMON PURPOSE

COMMON PURPOSE

How Great Leaders Get Organizations to Achieve the Extraordinary

JOEL KURTZMAN

JOSSEY-BASS
A Wiley Imprint
www.josseybass.com

Published by Jossey-Bass

A Wiley Imprint

989 Market Street, San Francisco, CA 94103-1741—www.josseybass.com

Jossey-Bass books and products are available through most bookstores. To contact Jossey-Bass directly call our Customer Care Department within the U.S. at 800-956-7739, outside the U.S. at 317-572-3986, or fax 317-572-4002.

Jossey-Bass also publishes its books in a variety of electronic formats. Some content that appears in print may not be available in electronic books.

Library of Congress Cataloging-in-Publication Data

Kurtzman, Joel.

Common purpose : how great leaders get organizations to achieve the extraordinary / Joel Kurtzman. — 1st ed.

p.cm.

Includes bibliographical references and index.

ISBN 978-0-470-49009-9 (cloth)

1. Leadership. 2. Organizational change. I. Title.

HD57.7.K867 2010

658.4'092—dc22

2009041345

Printed in the United States of America

FIRST EDITION

HB Printing   10 9 8 7 6 5 4 3 2 1

CONTENTS

To Karen Warner, who teaches leaders how to lead

FOREWORD

By Marshall Goldsmith

Major changes have occurred in the world of organizations since the late 1990s. In fact, not since the Industrial Revolution have we seen such rapid and significant change in the world of organizations. These changes, brought on by such forces as globalization, the development of technology, and their impact on our societies, are becoming increasingly evident as we progress into the 21st century.

As the century unfolds, new realities are becoming clearer. Multinational mega-organizations are emerging, and organizations are consolidating through mergers and acquisitions, yet simultaneously, smaller and mid-sized companies do flourish. New models of leadership are blossoming, some with unfounded success. For instance, focusing on working better as teams and empowering those closest to the customers to make important decisions have led to great accomplishments.

But who is to say what model will work for any specific organization, industry, or team? Because of the diversity of customers, technologies, and areas of operation, companies can't produce just workbooks and manuals anymore. The world is too big, too changing, and too varied. As a result, leaders and their followers must make the right decisions on their own because they have internalized the organization's mission, values, strategy, and brand.

Companies that understand this hire leaders who pay as much attention to developing the culture of the organization as to the individuals who make up the organization. They hire leaders who focus on common purpose—building a sense of inclusiveness within the organization where people know what to do and why, and understand what the organization stands for—and stand with it!

In *Common Purpose: How Great Leaders Get Organizations to Achieve the Extraordinary,* Joel Kurtzman takes his many years of research, personal observation, interviews, and interactions with leaders and distills them into one critical concept that is the essence of good leadership: excellent leaders create a feeling of "we" among the members of their group, team, or organization—they do this in order that the organization, now aligned around a common set of goals, is nearly undefeatable by any circumstance or competitor.

The road to common purpose in leaders and leadership is not an easy one. This book provides a road map to stay on that journey—and to succeed along the way.

Life is good.

Marshall Goldsmith is the best-selling author of *What Got You Here Won't Get You There, Succession: Are You Ready?,* and *MOJO.*

INTRODUCTION:
NO ONE LEADS ALONE

Since the end of World War II, tens of thousands of books, articles, studies, and theories have been developed on the topic of leadership, with thousands more coming out each year. People are fascinated by the subject and want to discover how they can become better leaders or rise to leadership-level positions. Authors and researchers have approached the topic from a wide variety of perspectives—business, politics, religion, community—and from disciplines like psychology, economics, and sociology. They've studied primate behavior, whale and dolphin pods, people in prison, native tribes living in the world's rain forests and savannas, CEOs, politicians, and sports figures.

And yet despite all this work, a consensus has so far failed to emerge with respect to what leadership is, how leaders develop, and—perhaps most important—how to become a more effective leader. Ideas about how to rise inside organizations run the gamut from, "It's all luck and politics," to "It's all hard work and preparation," to "You've got to generate your own internal PR," to "There's no limit to how high you can climb as long as you don't care who gets the credit." Others point to the power of teams and team building and of finding the right team to join. And still others say you have to select a few choice assignments for yourself and then shine. As a result, the appetite for ideas that provide answers to the puzzle of leadership is almost insatiable.

This book, which is the result of years of research and hundreds of interviews and personal observations and interactions with leaders, provides an answer to the leadership question. But in my opinion it is different from all those leadership books and studies already on the shelf because it demonstrates that the heart and soul of leadership is the creation of *common purpose.* Common purpose is a new concept.

What is common purpose? To me, it is that rare, almost palpable experience that happens when a leader coalesces a group, team, or community into a creative, dynamic, brave, and nearly invincible *we.* It happens the moment the organization's values, tools, objectives, and hopes are internalized in a way that enables people to work tirelessly toward a goal. Common purpose is based on a simple idea: the leader is not separate from the group he or she leads. Rather, the leader is the organization's glue—the force that binds it together, sets its direction, and makes certain that the group functions as one. Common purpose is rarely achieved, but I have seen it when a leader is able to bring about results that are outsized, measurable, and inspiring.

My interest in this topic was kindled long before I became editor-in-chief of the *Harvard Business Review,* where one in seven articles submitted to the magazine, out of more than four thousand articles submitted each year, was about leadership. My interest was provoked long ago by Warren Bennis when I was an editor, reporter, and columnist at *The New York Times.*

Bennis, a professor of business at the University of Southern California and a long-time student of leadership, had written many books on the topic. As a journalist, I did most of *The New York Times's* CEO interviews and also interviewed a great many politicians and military leaders. Because of those interviews, I became fascinated with how certain people were able to motivate the troops (literally and figuratively) day in and day out.

One day when Bennis was in New York, I asked him how leaders inspire and encourage followers (for lack of a better word) to take action. How did someone like Dwight D. Eisenhower, for example, motivate 160,000 soldiers to cross the English Channel and storm Normandy's beaches underneath a constant hail of lead? Or, more mundanely, how does Sam Palmisano, chairman and CEO of IBM, ensure that the company's 388,000 employees are working together, and not just for themselves? How do leaders make certain the individuals in their organizations are contributing value to the bottom line? What enables leaders to keep their people aligned? And what prevents chaos from breaking out? In short, how does a leader transform individuals from *me* into *we*? And why do some leaders fail?

The answer Bennis gave was clever. Leaders don't do it alone, he said. Good leaders are not outsiders who cheer on a group. They are part of that group, integrated deeply into its fabric and emotional life. "Great generals may climb the ranks," he said, "but they are still soldiers. Someone who views himself as an outsider or as above the other members of the group can almost never succeed as a leader."

"So there must be a sense of identity and connection between leaders and led?" I asked.

"Yes," Bennis replied. "If there isn't a deep connection, a real fit, the leader will fail. Quite literally," he continued, "when there isn't a fit, the group will either eject the leader or destroy itself in the attempt."

I had noticed as much. During my tenure at *The New York Times* (which is to say, the 1990s), no one was able to ascend to the masthead unless he or she had been a reporter. To obtain any real power in the newsroom, you had to show the paper's notebook-toting reporters that you understood the demands of their job, knew how it was done, and had done it yourself. Reporters might have earned their chops at another newspaper like the *Wall Street Journal.* Where they earned them was not that important. What mattered was *that* they earned them. Editors, brilliant though they might be, could never earn the kind of credibility that came from working a beat. Connecting with the group you lead means demonstrating you are part of the group, understand its challenges, can do its jobs, and can stand the pressure and the heat. These attributes cannot be faked.

These requirements are not limited to newspapering. At New York Life, a large life insurance company, no one rises very far without having spent at least some time sitting at a stranger's kitchen table selling life insurance. At UPS, almost every CEO started behind the wheel of a big brown van or working in a warehouse. Procter & Gamble, one of the oldest, most successful, and most admired companies (it was founded in 1837), has never brought in an outsider as CEO.

These examples may sound quaint, but the truth is that no one can succeed as a leader without creating a deep connection with those he or she leads. And this connection must be genuine. The leader and the followers must feel like the *we* of a group.

Such feelings cannot be manufactured out of thin air. They must be genuine and heartfelt. And yet every leader I interviewed, worked with, or have met over the years has confided that the connection between a leader and the people they lead is fragile and can be broken at any time. Leaders must renew their connections to their groups, and they must do it every day. If they don't, and instead take these bonds for granted, the group will reject them. Peak performance comes only when the leader and the group function as one.

Rejecting a Leader

I once consulted to a global automobile parts manufacturing company based in Detroit. The company designed and produced gears, brakes, axels, electronics, and lots of other components that make cars run. It had factories around the world and sales in excess of $15 billion; it also had almost no profits and a falling stock price.

I went in with a team from a consulting firm to try to create efficiencies that would save the company money and boost earnings. It was consulting 101. The consulting team had done similar projects around the world. But it just wasn't working at this company, and my job was to find out why.

From the moment I entered the company's glass-and-steel headquarters, I sensed something was wrong. You could practically feel it in the air and see it in the downcast faces of almost everyone who worked there—from guards at the security desk, to the people on the assembly lines, to the accountants in the offices, to the men and women working the forklifts. You could feel it when you walked into the cafeteria. The mood was glum.

It took a single meeting with the chairman/CEO to see what was wrong. He was amiable, able, and successful. He had a power office, wore a power tie, and played great golf. He had two secretaries and a tricked-out airplane to fly him around the world.

But he was a salesman who had ascended the ranks of what was an engineering and manufacturing company that had a distinct engineering and manufacturing culture and mind-set. As a salesman, he couldn't connect with the men and women who actually made the stuff he sold. There was mistrust all around. And as if that weren't enough, the chairman/CEO was at war with the popular head of manufacturing—a highly experienced engineer—over how to cut costs. Everyone knew a war was being waged, and everyone seemed to be rooting against the chairman/CEO.

Why didn't they trust the chairman/CEO? Most people in the company felt the sales force was not committed to anything but sales. They didn't care if the products the company made were the world's best or worst. All they cared about were their commissions. But the engineering and manufacturing teams did care. They took pride in their designs, the quality of their products, their low defect rates, their cutting-edge ideas. They were a Six Sigma shop all the way.

To rise above his predicament, we advised the CEO that he had to assert his authority, demonstrate leadership, and find a powerful, even symbolic way to create a connection with the people from the engineering and manufacturing side of the business. We suggested that he have a heart-to-heart talk with the head of manufacturing—one of those "we're either in this together, or you're going to have to find yourself another job" discussions. And we also advised that he put a short time limit on how long he'd wait for the head of manufacturing to demonstrate to people loyal to him that he and the chairman/CEO saw eye-to-eye.

"If you don't do that," we said, "even though you are the chairman/CEO, the company might reject you."

Needless to say, the chairman/CEO didn't like what we said. "This entire company reports to me," he answered. "And so does the board."

Unfortunately, the chairman/CEO followed his own path. He didn't confront the head of manufacturing and never tried to connect with the troops. He didn't demonstrate his appreciation for the design and quality of the products. In fact, he did the opposite. In a discussion with someone from manufacturing, he said there was such a thing as "too much quality," a statement that was repeated throughout the firm. To the CEO, too much quality was synonymous with too much expense.

The mood of the company, along with its stock price, continued to founder. Six months later, the board in closed session summoned up its courage and dismissed the chairman/CEO, replacing him with a gruff, no-nonsense engineer everyone seemed to love. In less than a year, the engineer turned the place around. A year after that, the company was acquired at a significant premium by another company. The failure of the original chairman/CEO to create a sense of common purpose cost him his job. Even worse, it was most likely the reason the company's stock had languished. Failing to create common purpose destroyed value.

Connecting doesn't simply mean bonding with those you feel comfortable with—a sales rep with other sales reps. It means bonding with the organization as a whole. In some ways, being the leader of an organization—any organization—is like being the mayor of a small town, as Meg Whitman, former chair and CEO of eBay, once said. There are ward bosses who have to be schmoozed, voters who have to be romanced, opponents who have to be neutralized, independents who have to be converted. The whole town has to feel at one with you if it is to operate at peak levels of performance.

LEADERS VERSUS LEADERSHIP

Leaders are people who rise to prominence. But *leadership* is different. Leadership is about what leaders *do*. A leader who mistakes one for the other can suffer a dangerous fall.

Leadership is akin to a contract between the leader and the group. To use a tired analogy, if leaders are the captains of the ship, they sign a contract with the board of directors (or its equivalent, depending on the leader's level in the organization) and also with those who are furling the sails, coiling the ropes, hoisting the anchors, and sweeping the decks. It's those people—the deckhands and swabbies—as much as the board who can eject any leader from his or her job.

The contract that leaders sign stipulates they are to select the destination; plot a course to it; arrive with crew, cargo, and ship intact; and put down mutinies should they occur along the way. If the wind changes, they have to tack. But if the seas rise, they are not free to change destinations. They are hired to achieve a goal, no matter the odds.

While some leaders have become legends (Jack Welch, Lou Gerstner, Harvey Golub, Andy Grove) they did not sign contracts to glorify their names or create personal legacies. That's for a different type of leader. And besides, they know that visibility often means vulnerability. Rather, the type of leader I am describing signs a contract to do a difficult and sometimes dangerous job: piloting a ship to an agreed-on goal. If a leader becomes famous for doing his or her job, that's great. But it's not the goal.

One excellent leader, George M. C. Fisher, a mathematician and engineer, led Motorola from the backwaters of business to its heights by investing in cell phone technology and computer chip manufacturing. The company's stock value soared under his leadership, and it plummeted when he left. Next, he went to Kodak, where he transformed that company from a sclerotic manufacturer of film and related products into a digital imaging company. In both instances, Fisher was successful, but he had to overcome longstanding corporate vested interests. In both instances, he also had to fight against powerful rivals (at Motorola, it was Intel, IBM, and Hitachi; at Kodak, it was Fuji Film).

When Fisher finished the job he signed on to do—position each company for the future—he quit. He left behind no statues in his own honor, no oil paintings of him in a suit, no corporate campus named after himself. There weren't any $50,000 coat racks or $1 million birthday parties. He just did his job.

LEADERSHIP GLUE

Great leaders not only must connect; they must develop a knack for sensing—for lack of a better word—the emotional tone of the group. True, there are incentives leaders can use like so many carrots and sticks. They can use money and other types of rewards, and they can use recognition, power, and promotions. Leaders can mete out punishments: dismissals, demotions, dressing-downs (the list is long). But these go only so far. Much more powerful than punishments or rewards is the way great leaders evoke the emotions of those they lead: love, hate, fear, courage, pride, empathy.

Not too long after Bill Clinton's term as president ended, I attended a small get-together with him and a few venture capital, high-tech, and media executives in Aspen. Here was a man still at the height of his powers who came to Aspen to discuss the situation in Rwanda with an interested and influential group (I was running a business at the time). But after a half-hour on that topic, one of the venture capitalists, a Republican, asked Clinton an off-topic question: Why were the Democrats so mean-spirited toward the Republicans? Granted, this was an off-the-wall, off-topic, and just plain strange question, given that Clinton was discussing Rwanda and what could be done to help Paul Kagame, Rwanda's president, save his nation. But the venture capitalist asked the question nevertheless.

Now, I admire Clinton's thoughtfulness, ability, and intelligence. But when he received that question, he became a different man. He pointed his finger at the questioner, his voice quivering as he recounted everything negative the Republicans had done to him. He asked rhetorical questions: *Can you imagine what it was like to be investigated for six years about Whitewater when there was nothing there?* He let loose with volleys of anger, invitations for empathy, even fear: *Do you know what they did to my wife, Hillary? Can you imagine the toll it took on her? The pain she suffered? The time she wasted on those baseless charges?*

Clinton, a charismatic, empathetic speaker, used his emotions the way an orchestra conductor uses his baton: to arouse, manipulate, and control. Watching him that afternoon for a full thirty minutes was like listening to a Wagner opera. Clinton's emotional pitch was intense. It was filled with rhythmic cadences, long outpourings, and deeply felt themes. It was an emotional tour de force and it had all fifteen of us spellbound—at first.

But then it became off-putting, and it started to make a number of us (especially those of us who liked Clinton) more than a little uncomfortable. Why? Because Clinton's operatic outburst was all about *him,* whereas great leaders use their command of emotions to make it all about *you,* all about *us.* And perhaps most important, Clinton's emotional outburst was way off-agenda. He had come to talk about Rwanda and ended up talking about himself. Worse, he had let someone else steal his agenda, shift the focus, and change the subject unproductively—something a leader must never do. For a man of Clinton's accomplishments, ability, and innate leadership skills, it was not his best day. Maybe he was jet-lagged; perhaps he was tired. But everyone knew he could have done far better.

COMMON PURPOSE

Great leaders motivate people by building a sense of inclusiveness, which is how they connect with and become accepted by the group. They create a sense of *we* by using their emotions as well as other tools—ideas, arguments, numbers, and so on—in strategic and disciplined ways. A leader's authority derives from effectively balancing what can only be called the near-schizophrenic task of being a genuinely accepted member of a group, while having sufficient detachment to constantly adjust course. To do that, leaders must be conscious about which emotions to display and when to display them. They must use their full set of leadership tools to create common purpose, which is how one person impels another to act without directing that other person's every move. Common purpose is what turns *me* into *we*.

Common purpose is a force you can almost feel. It animates great companies and great movements, and it can be summoned to propel a politician forward. When cared for, nurtured, and protected, it produces an almost palpable sense of *we* that can be felt inside the company. It is the feeling that we're all in this together and that we all know and understand what to do, why we're here, and what we stand for.

Examples of common purpose organizations are exceedingly rare, but they can be found in all sectors and for each generation. NASA's Apollo Program is a perfect example. NASA achieved an impossibly audacious goal at the urging of President Kennedy in 1961. Kennedy challenged NASA to put men on the moon and bring them back safely, and to do so within a decade's time. Against all odds and against high levels of danger, NASA achieved its goal while the entire world watched.

This was more than just a big job well executed. Kennedy's bold vision unified a nation and an organization around a goal. How audacious was it? In 1961, the United States was far behind the Soviet Union in the so-called space race. NASA was only three years old and was able only to shoot a man up into space and down into the sea, whereas the Russians had already put a cosmonaut into orbit around the earth. American rockets were primitive, computers were barely existent, and the word *astronaut* was still new. Not only that, but in 1961, there was no design for a rocket that could make it all the way to the moon. What made NASA succeed was that it put aside all its doubts and limitations, took out a clean sheet of paper, and decided as a group to succeed.

More recently, Pixar developed common purpose when it created an entirely new art form, a powerful culture, and an enterprise value equal to more than $1 billion per film—ten times the value of its nearest rival. Pixar created sufficient common purpose to develop its technology on a shoestring and survive ego battles with its alliance partner, the Walt Disney Company, all the while creating movies the entire world wanted to watch. Not only that, but when Pixar was finally sold to Disney in 2006 for $7.4 billion, one of the reasons that the venerable old mouse (as in Mickey) bought the digital company was to change Disney's culture from stale and traditional to cutting edge and digital.

Google is famously a common purpose organization, having seeped into the global vernacular as a verb. It is a powerful and pioneering competitor with an outsized mission and an inspiring leadership team that brings together head and heart in the service of higher goals.

Harvey Golub, the legendary chairman and CEO of American Express until 2001, was responsible for turning around what had been a moribund company (when it was headed by James Robinson III) and making it into one of the world's most successful and admired firms. He did it, he once said, by doing only one thing: making all eighty thousand employees understand what the company's brand stood for. "If everyone understands that," he said, "we won't need thick employee manuals, management training programs, or pricing schedules for the services we sell. Everyone will instinctively do the right thing." Through common purpose, he was able to make the company's mission statement its brand, having employees and customers buy in to the American Express ethos of being the world's most respected service brand.

Making the Goal

Common purpose is the goal of great leaders and great leadership. It is the way a group of free agents is transformed into a cohesive, orderly group—an organization—aligned around a common set of goals in a way that makes defeat almost impossible. Common purpose made it possible for Burt Rutan's SpaceShipOne team to win an Ansari X Prize and for the success of the iPod. Common purpose infused early Obama supporters with hope and older Martin Luther King Jr. supporters with a dream. It sent men to the moon, and it was behind the heroism of the rescuers who entered the Twin Towers even as the buildings were coming down. Common purpose is not just a feeling; it is a force.

The easiest way to create a sense of *us* or *we*—unfortunately—is to create the specter of *them*. Almost any leader can do this.

Building *we* on the backs of *them* is what created unity among squabbling Germans as the Weimar Republic disintegrated and the Nazis rose to power. On a different level altogether, when Microsoft was still a young company, it built its cohesive and aggressive culture out of a sense of *us versus them,* and *we* are smarter than *you.*

But like almost every other instance, when motivations are based on an us-versus-them theme, Microsoft's culture ended up veering out of control. The company faced lawsuits, Justice Department inquiries, threats of breakup, and restrictions imposed on it by the European Union. Backlashes against Microsoft were rampant. Large clients like the governments of Germany and Spain defected to open source software. Venture capital firms created anti-Microsoft funds, strategies, and even a cluster of linked, anti-Microsoft high-tech firms. Linux and other standards arose to counter Microsoft's marketplace power. All of this opposition forced the company to change—at great cost and not a moment too soon. And while us-versus-them is a shortcut toward common purpose, it can also be a stepping-stone to chaos, doom, and organized opposition.

For leaders, there is only one way that's worse than binding a group together using an us-versus-them strategy: coupling it with the wrong incentives. When leaders pursue higher goals, the results have been almost magical. For example, among environmentalists, the danger of a warmer tomorrow has created common purpose among a number of long-time foes. Carl Pope, leader of the Sierra Club, has joined forces with GE Nuclear Power, a company that was once on the club's worst-company list. To understand the unlikelihood of this alliance, all you have to do is recall GE's responsibility in dumping dioxin and other toxins into the Hudson River, a substance banned in 1977, and remember the way environmentalists like Pope used to feel about nuclear power. At the same time, and for the same reasons, Boone Pickens, an iconoclastic billionaire and rabid Republican (he funded the "Swift Boat Veterans for Truth" ads against John Kerry), is now a supporter of Al Gore's environmental initiatives and has met cordially with President Obama.

But higher goals do not necessarily mean cosmic goals. At Carnival Cruise Lines, the world's largest cruise ship operator, the organization's common purpose is to create an experience for its customers that they will remember forever. This goal is repeated to all employees almost daily by Micky Arison, Carnival's chairman and CEO. In every way he can, Arison reminds his employees that their customers are hard-working people who have set aside a week or two a year for fun. Everything the organization does is aligned around fulfilling their customers' goal.

COMMON PURPOSE

Chapter One

THE LEADERSHIP DISCONNECT

THE END OF HIERARCHY

A major disconnect exists today on the topic of leadership. I have heard senior leaders in business, government, and nonprofit organizations talk about the need to push decision making down in their organizations. They do this with the goal of making their organizations more responsive to their customers and constituencies and more competitive against rivals. Rather than wait until a problem moves up through the management levels, quality- and quick-response-minded organizations need people who can solve problems and pursue opportunities as soon as they arise. Minimizing response time has never been more important in an organization.

And yet while organizations need leaders at every level and in every function if they are to quicken their response time, senior executives still talk and, even worse, think in terms of leaders, followers, subordinates, and direct reports. Although these executives might espouse the value of flatness, they still think in hierarchical terms.

Just as bad, most of today's management literature and many management education and training programs continue to divide the world into leaders and followers. Not only is this not actionable (how can people at every level and in every function solve problems

1

as soon as they arise if they do not have the authority to do so?), it creates confusion, a great deal of organizational second-guessing, and anxiety. How people think about leadership determines the results they get. Even better, how people think about leadership determines *if* they get results.

POOR LEADERSHIP, POOR RESULTS

Shortly after the terrible events of September 11, 2001, I was at a meeting where FBI director Robert Mueller explained why his agency was unable to act on important information it had in advance of the terrorist plot. Mueller admitted that agents within the FBI knew the names of the 9/11 plotters and even their whereabouts. The agents who had this information tried to alert their superior that an attack was imminent and that an organizational response must be prepared. And yet, as history shows, the FBI and other governmental security organizations failed to do anything at all.

In explaining his organization's lapses, Mueller said that in the culture of the FBI, agents with information are not authorized to act on that information. If they know something is imminent, they must send what they know up through the FBI's chain of command to people with decision-making authority. Because the FBI operates in a dangerous world, the chain of command is rigidly constructed to prevent the organization from acting on erroneous information.

But in the case of the FBI, no action was taken because in a hierarchy, the people at the top, who are expected to be the most knowledgeable, tend to look at information supplied by their subordinates with condescension. If something as important and dreaded as a terrorist plot were really under way, the people at the top think they would surely be aware of it. And so information vital to preventing a terrorist plot was transmitted into one of the FBI's many organizational black holes, unable to be acted on in time.

Later, in another organizational context, an experienced accountant, Sherron Watkins, who was working at Enron, signaled to the chairman of that organization, Ken Lay, that something was wrong with the company's many partnerships and the manner in which they were kept off the company's books. But rather than acting on his subordinate's information by taking it to the board, Lay chose to ignore Watkins. If something were really wrong, he reasoned, surely he, as chairman, would have known it. After all, Lay was the man who turned a humble Texas energy company into the darling of Wall Street.

Had Lay listened to the insights and warnings of an underling, he could have prevented what became the world's largest bankruptcy up to that time. Later still, more than two years before the onset of one of the worst financial crises ever, I heard Lewis Ranieri warn a room full of leaders in the banking, investment, private equity, hedge fund, and insurance industry that the subprime mortgage market was about to blow up and that when it did, the consequences would be catastrophic.

Why should the people in the room have paid attention to Ranieri? Because he was one of the inventors of mortgage-backed securities, the very product that was about to explode and bring down the world's financial system. The penalty for not paying attention to Ranieri was harsh, and many leaders in that room lost their jobs, their money, and even their institutions. They did so because they believed themselves wiser than the amiable and slightly disheveled inventor of these powerful but misused financial tools. After all, though Ranieri invented a market, he was an outsider, and they prided themselves on knowing that market far better than he did.

THINKING LEADS TO RESULTS

Not paying heed to a warning or creating structures that stifle action once a warning is sounded is not the only leadership lapse that can occur when people in organizations continue to think in terms of leaders and followers.

Strangely, at Enron, Lay and Jeffrey Skilling, the company's now-imprisoned CEO, often discussed the fact that Enron was a flat organization where every person was either an entrepreneur or a potential entrepreneur. They gave interviews, including one to a coauthor and me in 2000, saying their company would become the world's largest firm, measured by market capitalization, because its people had sufficient autonomy to start new businesses and pursue new initiatives within the firm. They called their model "loose/tight": be loose with regard to controlling people and tight with regard to controlling finances. The model might actually have worked if the firm had been run by an honest CEO or had its chairman listened to Watkins's warnings.

Both the financial industry and the FBI pride themselves on their ability to ferret out information and act on it. And yet the top-down structure of these organizations obstructed the flow of vital information, making it impossible for people to act. Why did they fail to act? Because despite their rhetoric regarding the need for flatness, these two organizations were designed and constructed, and people were rewarded and given authority to act, in traditional hierarchical terms.

MISSED OPPORTUNITIES

Inaction in the face of new knowledge or information is only one of the consequences of hierarchy when the people at the top are too busy, too insulated, or too wise to pay attention. Missed opportunity is another. It is extremely difficult to list the number of instances in which poor leadership led to an organization's inability to seize an opportunity because there are simply too many instances in which that is the case.

Tragically, poor leadership tends to perpetuate itself, which explains why once great organizations slowly wither and die. As Joe Griesedieck, vice chairman and managing director of CEO services at Korn/Ferry, the world's largest search firm, told me, A players pick other A players with whom they surround themselves and from whom they build their teams. But B players pick B and even C players to prevent their leadership from being challenged. Over time, B players are succeeded by the B and then C players they picked. And since leaders in hierarchical organizations can't really be challenged, the tyranny of the B player is preserved. As a result, once great organizations wither and die. Missing out on opportunities is as much a killer of organizations as failing to pay attention to bad news.

One long-lived company's experience might prove instructive. Western Union, founded in 1851, commercialized the telegraph. In 1865, at the end of the American Civil War, the first war in which the telegraph played a role, Western Union was America's largest and most valuable communications company. In 1884, it was one of the original stocks in the Dow Jones Industrial Average, having built a nationwide communications infrastructure. And then it went to sleep.

Western Union was organized from the top down, like most other companies of its time. All strategic decisions and capital allocation decisions were made at the very top. Western Union's leaders could not be challenged. They were experienced people, from similar backgrounds. They had inherited a company of substance, which they were determined to preserve. And they were suspicious of outsiders and of new ideas.

In 1879 a young, Massachusetts-based educator and high-tech inventor, Alexander Graham Bell, attempted to interest Western Union in one of his inventions: the telephone. He argued that with his patents and its nationwide infrastructure of telegraph wires, the company could quickly be transformed into something new and potentially far more valuable: a national telegraph *and* telephone company.

The never-before-challenged leaders of Western Union huddled together and examined Bell's patents, which they collectively deemed "no big deal." Of course, we now know Bell's patents were the most valuable in all of business history and went on to form the basis of the U.S. and global telephone industries. Those patents led to the creation of the Bell Telephone System, the American Telephone and Telegraph Company (AT&T), and many other companies. For nearly a century, the companies Bell founded were the world's most valuable, enriching millions of investors who owned their stocks.

After it had passed on the telephone, Western Union was offered another new invention: radio. With radio, information could travel around the globe instantly, reaching communities everywhere, not to mention ships at sea and airplanes high above the earth. But Western Union passed on radio too.

Later, in the late 1930s, Western Union glanced at another new technology: television. Some of its suppliers had decided to produce TV sets and TV production equipment, but the leaders at Western Union once again declined to participate, preferring instead to focus on what made them money *then*—delivering telegrams and transferring money—rather than what might make them money in the future.

Later still, Western Union observed the introduction of the Internet and briefly flirted with the idea of becoming a player in that burgeoning field. And why not? With its wire-and-microwave-based infrastructure, Western Union could have become an important carrier of packets of digital Internet traffic. But in the end, Western Union failed to invest in the Internet.

Finally, in the early 1970s, Western Union watched as cellular telephone technology was developed by Motorola and then commercialized in the mid-1980s by AT&T, one of Bell's companies.

Again, Western Union's infrastructure could have supported this technology. But the company decided not to invest. Western Union kept its network and its company intact, but failed to take advantage of decades of progress and change.

Today Western Union continues to exist, but it is limping along on the verge of extinction, saddled with debt, having been taken over, sold, and resold several times. And rather than growing, this old firm has spent most of its long life in slow decline. Today, as in 1871, Western Union's largest (and now sole) business is transferring money.

Western Union's leadership never missed an opportunity to miss an opportunity. Quite literally, they passed on the most significant technological advancements of the past 130 or so years. One can only imagine how different things might have been for this once-stellar firm if its insular leadership, and insulating leadership structure, had been open to new ideas. What if it had invested in the telephone? Radio? TV? The Internet? Cellular technology? What if it had built its business around innovation?

How many other organizations are in the same boat as Western Union, missing opportunities, failing to innovate, resistant to change, led by a cloistered assortment of B and C players? How many organizations turn away from the future even when it knocks at the door? Sadly, the answer is *far too many*.

LEADERSHIP DETERMINES RESULTS

These examples represent only a tiny handful of organizations whose leaders have created extreme vulnerabilities, stifled growth, and limited reach and caused damage. A comprehensive list of organizations whose leadership has done similar damage would be long.

But leadership matters not just when it comes to preventing calamities and seizing opportunities. It matters when it comes to retaining talent, an organization's most precious resource. Richard Boyatzis, a professor of business at Case Western Reserve University and a noted researcher regarding individuals in organizations, told me in an interview that some firms actually become emotionally toxic places to work because of the way they are led.

Leaders within toxic organizations create cultures, or allow toxic cultures to develop, that harm the organization's talent. Badly led, toxic organizations not only dispirit the individuals who remain in place (the best people usually leave), they create environments of low productivity, low expectations, poor morale, and flagging creativity. And it doesn't end there. Poorly led organizations lose their resiliency. Not only that, but Boyatzis's research suggests that working in this type of organization can produce measurable physiological symptoms among the workforce. In other words, according to Boyatzis, some organizations are so badly led, so stifling to the dreams of employees, so damaging to their abilities and passions, that they can take a toll on their employees' health.

If every organization at the moment of its inception begins with big dreams, high hopes, and lofty goals, why do some sink into oblivion? Why do once great organizations fall into decline? The answer can be found in the way they are led.

A NEED TO ACHIEVE

Individuals are much more than cogs in the wheel of commerce. We've known that for decades. People are complex. They have hopes, fears, ambitions, dreams, and wide-ranging talents. Most people want to express themselves and contribute, and they want to belong.

For decades, studies around the world have confirmed that the overwhelming majority of people work for more than a paycheck. They work to find fulfillment, self-expression, and a chance to add value. Study after study has shown that making the big bucks, which is important to a small set of individuals, particularly those on Wall Street, is not usually at the top of the list for most people. What is at the top of their list? Being part of a winning team in a winning organization that has a mission.

Research confirms that human beings working within organizations want to make a difference and be heard and recognized for their achievements. Even in clandestine organizations like the CIA, which attracts a type of person who likes (and probably needs!) to stay in the shadows and out of the limelight, employees crave recognition. Awards and even medals are given to employees who perform at their utmost, even if they work inside organizations dedicated to secrecy, discretion, and staying out of sight.

The need to be recognized for their achievements and for doing a good job is so universal that individuals routinely spend multiples of the monetary value of a prize in order to win it. The Ansari X Prize for space awarded $10 million to the first team to build and launch on its own, and without government help, a spacecraft capable of carrying three people to a hundred kilometers above the earth's surface, twice within two weeks.

That prize was awarded in 2004 to a team of engineers, technicians, and aircraft and space entrepreneurs led by the space-and-airframe design pioneer Burt Rutan and financed by Microsoft cofounder Paul Allen. The team built and launched a craft called SpaceShipOne. How much did the team spend to win the $10 million prize? About $25 million.

The need to be recognized is universal. When the Defense Advanced Projects Research Agency announced in 2004 that it was awarding a $2 million prize to the first group that could build a robotized car from scratch that could drive itself on a 142-mile course through a California desert, 195 teams entered the competition. They came from thirty-six states and represented thirty-five universities, three high schools, dozens of companies, and a number of individuals. To win the prize, which was awarded in 2005, competitors collectively spent $100 million.

It's not just spies, space geeks, and robot nerds who need recognition. On a far smaller scale, one has only to glance at Web sites that auction restored, and sometimes prize-winning, vintage automobiles, airplanes, boats, and other items. Almost without exception the cost of restoring these items exceeds their asking and final sale prices.

Why did people spend so much to restore these items? It's not that these projects got out of hand. It's that once people begin work on a project for which they are fully responsible and in control, they do not restrain themselves from doing the best jobs they can.

The need to do our best and be recognized for it is not something that develops. It's inherent in us. Between them, the Girl Scouts and Boy Scouts, and their sister and brother organizations like the Brownies and Cub Scouts, offer several hundred types of achievement and recognition awards, such as merit badges (boys) and bronze, silver, and gold awards (girls), in addition to leadership awards, levels, and ranks. These programs, for boys and girls roughly between the ages of eight and eighteen, have had hundreds of millions of members from around the world, beginning early in the last century. To receive awards of excellence and be recognized for their accomplishments, boys and girls must work hard. And, unlike school, which is compulsory, these programs are voluntary and require hours of preparation, work, and study.

I am not a sociologist or anthropologist, but I have observed firsthand leaders in action in all types of organizations around the world. Over the past several decades, I have discussed leadership with hundreds of experts around the world, and regardless of sector or nationality, certain commonalities have emerged.

Most people, of all ages and in all positions, want to do their best, contribute their utmost, and be recognized for having done so. If they are not doing their best, point your finger at their leaders—the people with power—and not at them. If people are willing, on their own and voluntarily, to devote time and money to express excellence, why aren't they more willing to do it at work? Why aren't they willing to sacrifice for their organization? The answer can be found by looking at who's in charge.

In my own observations of organizations, I have seen that far too many leaders keep people back, retard their progress, and blunt their enthusiasm and their edge. Why would any leader do such a thing, deliberately or not? Too many leaders hoard power and so restrict the ability of people to make decisions. People tend to do what is expected of them. Expect very little, and that's what you're likely to get. But when leaders refuse to distribute power to their teams, their organizations, or their firms, they are really creating a situation in which ultimately they will get little help from the people who are around them since those people will not feel at liberty to act. Not only that, but by hoarding power, leaders create environments of second-guessing and mistrust, conditions that rarely are associated with success.

Chapter Two

THE NEW RULES OF EMPLOYMENT

MUTUAL MISTRUST

From 1999 to 2005, when I was a Global lead partner for thought leadership at PricewaterhouseCoopers, I conducted an annual survey of CEOs from around the world. The release of the survey's results was always a big event and usually took place at the World Economic Forum annual meeting at Davos, Switzerland. The media were always present.

Each year the survey focused on one or more themes: business investment trends, whether CEOs were bullish or bearish about the future, if companies were likely to increase or decrease their hiring, how they viewed the financial markets—whichever issues were top-of-mind for the world's business leaders at the time. Dozens of interviewers would speak to the CEOs on the phone and in some cases meet with them in person to gather the data.

In 2005, I noticed something startling in the data as they rolled in. It has been well documented through long-running surveys, such as the Harris and Roper polls, that among employees and the population in general, there has been a growing, and now deep-seated, mistrust of top leaders in companies, especially with regard to the issue of CEO pay, estimated to be as high as four hundred times the pay of frontline workers for some companies, according to United for a Fair Economy, a nonprofit group, and the Corporate Library, a corporate governance group. But the 2005 survey indicated that CEOs also had begun mistrusting their employees. Specifically, CEOs were skeptical regarding the advice they received from employees, worried about how well their employees managed risks, and wondered whether the financial figures they received from employees were trustworthy.

Think how far we've fallen. Think what that means for most businesses. Somehow, despite the advice and research from the world's best business thinkers, CEOs and their employees have managed to create an environment in which some of the most important relationships have turned toxic.

Think back to the clubby (but largely mythical) good-old-boy business era of the 1950s and 1960s when CEOs were supposed to be paternalistic people who knew everything about the companies they ran and were supported by long-serving, loyal staffs known for their honesty, integrity, and humility. This view (which I am articulating in the extreme) was the old compact between organizations and the people who worked in them. The organization provided job security for the employee, and trust abounded. Employees, in return, bled blue if they worked for IBM; bled yellow if they worked for Caterpillar; and bled red if they worked for Coca Cola. The relationship was reciprocal and long term.

Now we are in an era in which CEOs are suspicious of their employees and dubious about the numbers they receive from them, and employees are equally mistrustful of the higher-ups and think they're greedy and (truth be told) not all that competent. This new compact represents an at-will relationship in which loyalty has gone by the wayside on the part of employers and employees alike. Just like the bygone era, the relationship is reciprocal: you don't trust me; I don't trust you. When times are good, employees vote with their feet. When times are difficult, they stay (if they can) but grudgingly.

You call that progress?

Today's organizational compact might seem like odd soil to plant the seeds of common purpose leadership. And yet in some ways, today's environment might actually be the best one in which to bring down mindless hierarchies and the many confusions it creates.

First, consider the circumstances today. Global leaders in finance, automobiles, real estate, construction, commodities, and other sectors have been brought to their knees. Many firms have faced bankruptcy and required government backing and bailouts and other types of strongly administered medicine. Some of the world's best-known brands have disappeared as independent companies. Some globe-girdling behemoths either shrank on their own to stay viable or were required to shrink through governmental action.

Why did it happen?

Many analysts say it happened because of easy credit, those nasty subprime loans, exotic financial practices like securitization, up-and-down oil and commodity prices, complicated-and-risky financial derivatives, and a world in which real estate was overbuilt. And while all that (and more) is true, these issues are more symptomatic of an underlying set of problems than the cause. In my view, bad—and, in many cases, abysmal—leadership within a large group of global institutions, governmental regulatory bodies, and in a variety of business and nonbusiness organizations is the real cause.

Bad leadership is not the fault of a single individual or even of a small group of individuals inside some flagging enterprise. Instead, it is baked into the structure of the organization. Bad leadership can endure over time and even over generations. Unless it is ruthlessly nipped in the bud by peers, boards of directors, shareholders, consumers, or others, bad leadership tends to perpetuate itself, albeit in a downward spiral.

Consider the sad case of GM, once one of the most admired companies in the world. The great management thinker Peter Drucker conducted a study of GM in 1943 that was published in 1946 as the book, *The Concept of the Corporation*. It went on to become one of the most important books on management ever written and elevated Drucker's name. At the time of the study, GM was one of the largest and most successful companies in the world. And yet as early as 1943, Drucker uncovered seeds of future leadership troubles, especially with regard to the way the company's leaders insulated themselves from outside criticism and complaints from customers and dealers.

What was GM's reaction to Drucker's work? GM's just-retired CEO and chairman, Alfred P. Sloan—the man who built GM's internal structure, product line, and dealer relationships and who was also responsible for its growth—refused to acknowledge that the book even existed. No one in 1943 took Drucker's warnings seriously.

A pity. Imagine if that once great company had developed a culture of responsiveness and openness. Imagine if instead of a culture where parts suppliers, dealers, customers, workers, and GM were locked in perpetual war, the company became a common purpose organization, more like Toyota, where those relationships are long term. At Toyota, rather than cutthroat negotiations between rivals, everyone, from supplier to manufacturer to dealer, is considered part of the same network working for the common good. There are examples of a time when a crucial Toyota supplier had a fire in its factory and other Toyota suppliers immediately picked up the slack and produced the missing parts for the factory that had burned. When the factory's fire damage was repaired, the suppliers resumed their old roles in the supply chain rather than trying to permanently take away the burned-out factory's business. What this shows is that it's not greed that runs through the Toyota system, but the goal of everyone's long-term economic and business survival.

Drucker's early observations and warnings about GM went unheeded, and although the company flourished in the 1950s and 1960s, its blind spots had begun to hamper its progress by the early 1970s. Japanese cars of superior quality entered the United States in a big way as gasoline prices soared. In addition, the environmental movement began to take hold.

Rather than realizing that people concerned about the environment and the high price of gasoline were either current or potential customers, GM reacted by ignoring these people or attempting to silence them. Environmentally conscious consumers, part of a fledgling movement in the 1970s, are in the mainstream now. And many of these people remember that GM urged the government to restrict imports on high-miles-per-gallon cars imported from Japan, fought against fuel economy standards, and dismissed environmental issues.

Not surprisingly, starting in the mid-1970s, GM began losing market share—and it has continued to lose market share for more than thirty years.

How could such a treasured institution slip so much, especially since the seeds of its slow downward spiral were observed as early as 1943? First, no one can attribute GM's woes to a thirty-year run of bad luck. Other automobile companies have prospered, notably the Japanese transplants and Ford, while GM has failed. Other firms from around the world may have been bowed by the global financial crisis, but not all of them needed governmental bailouts the way GM did. Italy's Fiat, for example, struggled through a period of debt, darkness, and irrelevance in the 1990s (it actually tried to sell itself to GM at one point), only to resurrect itself as a powerhouse company when its leadership changed. And when Fiat resurrected itself, it purchased Chrysler's asset in 2009 from a private equity firm, Cerberus Capital Management, which had purchased them in 2007, from Daimler-Chrysler, the German parent of Mercedes-Benz. Under Daimler's ownership, Chrysler had found itself starved for investment and suffering from an exodus of talent. Under Cerberus, the financial crisis took its toll, and the wrong leaders were put in place. When Fiat took over, it did so as a savior.

In my view, GM's problems are really leadership problems: either GM's leaders did not see what they needed to do see (one of the biggest sins in business), or they chose to ignore what they saw. What else would explain how GM's former chairman and CEO, Rick Wagoner, could hop on his private jet in late 2008 to fly to Washington, D.C., to ask Congress for a taxpayer-funded bailout?

It's not that traveling by private jet is a despicable act. CEOs of global companies have to cover a lot of ground, and often they must do it in a hurry. In some cases, a private plane is the best (indeed the only) option they have available. And in good times, when a company is growing, no one would put up a fuss. But in the middle of a financial crisis? When you're going to Washington to ask for taxpayer money to bail out decades of incompetent leadership?

Not only that, but the congressional hearings GM and its U.S.-based counterparts were attending were highly charged and politicized. Surely someone inside GM should have been aware of the tide of public opinion and how closely they were being scrutinized.

If no one at GM told Wagoner he should have flown coach on a commercial jet, it represents a serious set of management flaws. No one helping prepare Wagner for the hearings was aware enough, cared enough, or was brave enough to deliver news like that to the boss. And if someone did tell Wagoner to take a commercial flight and he ignored it, that is just as bad. Either way, the tiny problem seed Drucker observed in 1943 grew into a mighty problem tree. Those problems ultimately cost Wagoner his job and led to his disgrace in 2009 when the Obama administration's task force on the automobile industry unceremoniously told him to leave.

Danger Signs at GM, Circa 1943, According to Peter Drucker

- Insularity of top executives
- Poor industrial relations
- Friction between GM and its dealer network
- Disdain for customers
- A refusal to pay attention to thoughtful outside criticism

Source: P. Drucker, *The Concept of the Corporation* (Edison, N.J.: Transaction Books, 1993. (Originally published in 1946)

This is not the first time GM has teetered on the brink. When it was in trouble in 1992, I was a columnist and business editor at *The New York Times.* GM's sales were plummeting, its bonds had been marked down, and its fortunes were flagging.

Back then, I asked James P. Womack, an MIT professor, student of mass production, and author of *The Machine That Changed the World,* to write a prescription for Detroit's wounded giant. Womack's opus was so good I gave him as much space as he needed to write about what he'd learned from his study of the global automobile industry, especially Japanese manufacturers like Toyota. He wrote an insightful prescription that he thought might save GM. He covered manufacturing, management, marketing, costs, and GM's labor problems.

When the piece appeared, it received a lot of attention. Back then, in the heyday of newspapers, some of the senior people at GM no doubt saw Womack's article. And while not everything Womack listed was actionable, most of his article hit the mark. Besides, as a professor, researcher, and study leader at MIT, the world's most respected engineering school, you might have expected he would have gotten a call from someone at GM to explain his views. After all, the company *was* struggling.

But when I called Womack a few days after the article appeared and asked him if he had heard from anyone at what was still the world's largest car company, he said he "hadn't heard a word." Then he added, "But I didn't expect to hear from them. No one at GM really believes an outsider can fathom the company."

I was disheartened to hear that Womack's advice had been ignored. It was a powerful and thoughtful article of analysis and (I'm told) was reprinted and circulated widely.

So who's to blame that such a thoughtful piece of analysis was ignored? The worker on the assembly line? The salesman in the showroom? The parts manufacturer? The midlevel managers? Or the leaders at the top?

Womack's prescription was not an only analysis regarding how to fix what was wrong. Many consulting firms worked at GM and offered their views, business professors wrote case studies, and journalists diagnosed the company's woes. Financial analysts carefully examined the company and called attention to its problems. Even Ross Perot, the iconoclastic billionaire, one-time presidential candidate, and GM board member, said the company's leaders were a disaster. For that reason, he quit GM's board.

Surely some of GM's leaders must have read some of these analyses. But they either read them with their eyes wide shut, or the structure of the firm was so rigid that no one—*no one!*—felt strong enough to place Womack's article, or any other article, book, study, or paper, under the noses of GM's leadership team. And if one of the company's top team happened across a piece on the company, it was never shared.

Unfortunately, GM is not in a class by itself. Just prior to the financial crisis, leaders at Bear Stearns, Merrill Lynch, Lehman Brothers, Royal Bank of Scotland, UBS, and others must have known that leveraging their companies thirty-five or more times was risky, yet they allowed it to happen. They must have understood that if you borrow thirty-five times your own money to buy a portfolio of subprime mortgages or derivatives or any other type of financial product, if the price of that portfolio falls by only 3 percent, you're wiped out. A 3 percent decline is not something that has occurred only rarely in finance. It's well within the normal range of market fluctuations. And yet these financial firms, packed with traders, analysts, and bankers (many with off-the-charts IQs), did not see anything wrong with such high levels of leverage.

One could certainly ask, "What was wrong with these people?" And what was wrong with institutions that suppressed the concerns of a few outliers who tried to get their institutions to behave more rationally? Surely someone at Lehman Brothers or Merrill Lynch or Bear Stearns who heard Louis Ranieri's criticism of the subprime market must have voiced concern. Surely someone at the world's largest financial institutions must have read the widely circulated work of economist Nouriel Roubini, who forecasted a financial meltdown two years before it happened?

And they did. They heard them, and they read them. And then they ignored them.

And what about the big home builders in the United States? Surely some smart leader at D. R. Horton, Pulte, Lennar, Centex, or KB Homes must have understood that if these firms could sell homes only by giving mortgages to people who couldn't pay for them, something might be amiss. Certainly the nation's largest home builders must have understood this. After all, these companies had been in business for decades—some for generations—and had operated in all business conditions and in all geographies. And yet leaders at these big companies continued to buy land, subdivide it into lots, and pour foundations far beyond what the market needed.

How could so many leaders have bankrupted or nearly bankrupted so many companies? How could so many independent firms have been so poorly led?

In each of these instances, organizations and even whole economic sectors were either structured to select the wrong people to lead or they were unable to provide good leaders with the right tools to prevent disaster. In many instances, like the case of GM, long-standing shifts occurred so that leaders were insulated or felt justified in ignoring circumstances outside their firms.

Given the disasters that befell these organizations, the world is ripe for a new model of leadership—one that is open to, and even seeks information from, inside and outside the firm and is capable of mobilizing the organization's strengths in pursuit of change. Surely given what the world is witnessing, we need leadership that is protective of what previous generations have built.

Richard Boyatzis made a profoundly important point in *Creating Value Through People:* "Poorly led organizations will not be able to attract or retain talented people." And this has been proven time and time again. If you were a young, bright, newly minted MIT, Stanford, Caltech, or Carnegie Mellon engineer, would you want to go to work at an organization that has been in decline for decades? Or would you prefer to start your career at a company that is open to new ideas? Would you want to go to work at an organization famous for the insularity of its bosses, or would you want to work in an organization where leaders are accessible and everyone, at all levels, is viewed as an equal member of the team?

ORGANIZATIONAL STRUCTURES

We must finally put an end to the tyranny of mindless hierarchy because today's work-at-will environment is actually creating the opportunity for a so-called adult work relationship: one in which mutual interests and responsibilities (between employer and employed) are the watchwords in the value-creating process.

Organizations are not people. They are designed, developed, modified, and (far too frequently) destroyed by human beings. The organizations that survive do so by allowing people to develop in ways that make them more productive and responsive to changes in the environment. Insularity, rigidification, and failing to adjust to change in the environment are forces that destroy organizations.

To think that organizational structures are somehow fixed, sacrosanct, or beyond reinvention is simply wrong. All organizations must be viewed as works in progress, like novels whose ending the author has not yet fashioned or does not even know.

Organizations are simply ways people have developed for achieving goals that are beyond the capability of an individual to accomplish alone. They are methods for aligning groups of people so they achieve common goals.

When an organization inhibits the ability of a group of people to achieve its goals, it must be reformed. When an organization consistently raises up leaders who suppress, demean, or nullify the productivity of others, swift action must be taken to right this situation. When organizations fail to pay attention to changes in the internal and broad external environments, when they miss critical shifts in markets, geographies, demographics, or in technology, they must be reformed at once.

Organizations themselves are mindless, so if people don't repair them, no one will. Organizations cannot fix themselves; only people can do that. Because organizations are human constructs, good leaders must always keep an eye on whether the organizations they lead inhibit or promote progress.

MUTUAL INTERESTS

Winston Churchill once said countries don't have friends; they have interests. The same is true of organizations and the people who work in them. In any period in which organizations have no qualms about firing people and individuals have no guilt about quitting, loyalty has been replaced by three types of interests:

- *Personal interest.* People want good salary and benefits packages, but they also want an opportunity to grow as people and as professionals, to be challenged, to accomplish goals, to work with an interesting group of people, and to add their capabilities to those of others. In addition, people want to be respected and, as leadership expert Jon Katzenbach writes in his book *Why Pride Matters More Than Money,* want to take pride in what they do.

- *Mutual interests.* Organizations and individuals need to create value, and they must do it together. If individuals don't do it, they leave the organization voluntarily or because of the decisions of others. If organizations can't create value, they come undone. The metrics regarding value are not abstract. They focus on growth and performance that continues to improve. Stasis is never acceptable. One consideration regarding mutual interests is that to grow and improve, individuals need to have access to their organization's full set of tools and capabilities.

- *Organizational interests.* Organizations may not be human, but their number one interest is survival. As such, they must be robust, agile, and responsive, not rigid. Furthermore, they must grant talented people freedom to improvise when the need arises. Organizations are coordinators of capabilities, allocators of resources, and the place where performance metrics are kept. They also keep values and goals alive and viable as people come and go.

The goal of good leadership is to balance these interests so that the organization continually gains ground.

KEEPING ORGANIZATIONS TOGETHER

Great organizations can endure many different types of tribulations if they are able to keep the interests aligned. I know this because I did a study for a client that focused on how successful organizations endure to become hundred-year-old firms. In doing this work, I contrasted long-lived, successful organizations with a comparable group of defunct companies that I called "R.I.P. companies," for rest in peace. How does a company like Procter & Gamble, founded in 1837, continue to be successful and grow, while Burma-Vita, founded in 1925, maker of Burma Shave, go extinct? Why did the Knickerbocker Trust Company, founded in 1884, go out of business, while Lazard Brothers, founded in 1848, survives and grows? I studied about a hundred companies for this project.

Among the hundred-year-old organizations I studied, I found that if the individual, mutual, and organizational interests were kept aligned, the organization had the capacity to survive almost anything. Companies flourished despite two world wars (and in two cases, the U.S. Civil War). They survived the Great Depression, a dozen or so recessions, and several periods of inflation, stagflation, bear markets, bull markets, and financial meltdowns. Companies survived changes in technology. Two companies I studied even withstood the untimely deaths of their founders.

By keeping these interests aligned, hundred-year-old firms remained scrappy, vibrant, and highly competitive beyond all expectations. They had cultures that made people feel part of something bigger, which made the people who worked there feel special. Hundred-year-old firms shared the wealth in ways that were deemed fair within their industry sectors. They valued talent. The individuals who worked in these organizations felt that they were growing and that the teams they were part of were filled with people they liked and learned from. In times of peril, when the organization's survival was at stake, the leaders did what they had to do to keep the firms viable. To greater or lesser degrees, successful, long-lived organizations had a sense of common purpose.

What brought about the demise of the R.I.P. companies? I found three elements common to all them: lack of common purpose, lack of common vision, and lack of common goals. The behaviors that were most devastating to these organizations were constant disagreements about future direction, infighting, faction-alism regarding strategy, and what can only be called internal confusion. These behaviors made people wonder whether the organization's leaders really understood where they were going and what they were doing. In addition, R.I.P. organizations were plagued by rigid management structures. In some organizations people were afraid to voice doubts about the direction the company was taking. These firms experienced breakdowns of trust.

There were no differences between hundred-year-old compa-nies and defunct companies with regard to technology, systems, methodologies, geographies, and even products. Had people in the defunct organizations been able to get their views to the senior-most team and had those senior people listened, some of these companies might have survived.

POWER TO THE PEOPLE

People have a need to be heard, to be respected, and to control their space. Great leaders—common purpose leaders—grant them their space, give them their trust, allow them responsibility, and present them with opportunities and resources to do their jobs. But great leaders also hold people accountable. In other words, great leaders treat the people they work with as adults, which the current employment compact supports.

When I say "giving people control of their space," I am not referring to something New Age. Rather, I am suggesting that people need authority to do what they need to do. If the individuals are CEOs, they need authority over the entire company. The people to whom CEOs report—the board and shareholders—must grant CEOs sufficient trust and authority to carry out their jobs. But boards and shareholders must also hold their CEOs accountable for results—and not just today's results. CEOs must make certain that the companies over which they have authority are capable of surviving into the future.

Giving people control over their space doesn't mean giving it to just the highest-ranking people. It applies to everyone in the organization, from the security personnel at the door, to the people answering the phones, selling products and services, and tallying the accounts. If you have a job, you should *have* that job! *Own* that job as long as you're in it!

Jean-René Fourtou, former CEO of the French chemical giant Rhône-Poulenc and later the CEO who turned around Vivendi Universal, once said to me that he got very upset when people would say, "At a meeting, it was decided that . . . " His answer was, "Meetings don't decide; people decide." In other words, at the companies Fourtou has led, there are no faceless, nameless functions and no committees that make decisions. People have responsibility and decision-making authority. People are the unit of accountability. From Fourtou's point of view, everyone in an organization is an individual in the fullest sense of the word.

"We try to respect people and their contributions," he told me. "But most of all, there is a sense that when they work in this company, they are members of a community. As members of a community, they have leverage to do things they could not do on their own. Within that community, people feel— or should feel—responsible and empowered and respectful of each other as individuals." From Fourtou's perspective, organizations should be thought of as vehicles that help people to get things done.

Fourtou has walked the walk and really has given authority, responsibility, and trust to people working in the organizations he has led. But few other senior leaders can make the same claim. Most leaders, as the CEO survey mentioned at the beginning of this chapter suggests, are too mistrustful of the people on whom they depend to give them enough authority to do their jobs. As a result, they continue to exert too much control over the people on their teams. By doing so, they create a climate of fear, second-guessing, and subpar performance. By overcontrolling the people with whom they work, leaders hamper the performance of the groups they lead.

And why should it be any other way? If you're not free to act, you won't act. If you can't make a decision without it being challenged or changed, you won't make a decision. If you can't allocate resources without it causing a stir, you won't allocate them. What sane person would?

THOSE WHO CONTRIBUTE, THOSE WHO DON'T

The unfortunate truth is that not everyone has the same ability, need for success, or motivation. Nor does everyone share the same motives when making their day-to-day decisions. While it might not be popular to say so, most of us can point to coworkers who are perpetually negative, difficult, lazy, dishonest, or simply incapable of performing their jobs or unwilling to do so. People in these categories deserve a chance or two to turn themselves around, but they don't deserve more than that.

Fourtou once told me that when he became CEO of Rhône-Poulenc, the majority of people in the organization supported him, though a small minority of senior managers opposed him. What Fourtou saw quickly was that the detractors—those people who constantly needed "one more explanation" for the course he wanted to take—took up far too much of his time and energy. They would argue with him, require special meetings, need extra explanations, and still not come around. More and more time and attention was siphoned off by these people.

It's not that Fourtou did not brook dissent. He did. In fact, he liked people to challenge his ideas and put forward their own. And when they were right, he changed course. But there was a small group at the company that always dissented—a small group that always disagreed with regard to strategy.

Fourtou's solution to this problem was brilliantly simple: he simply stopped giving time and attention to the perpetual naysayers. He cut them off. After a relatively short time without receiving Fourtou's attention, most of the naysayers shifted their positions and changed their attitudes. They still challenged many of his decisions, but they did it in constructive, creative ways. Fourtou rewarded them for having changed by giving them the authority they needed to do their jobs. He bore them no ill will.

But that still left Fourtou with a small group of naysayers: people who couldn't be any other way but negative, did not like him, or could not be persuaded to align their goals with his. With this group, Fourtou was brutal: he let them go.

Once you discover that some negative people cannot rid themselves of their negativity, they must be allowed to find their purpose, passion, and opportunities elsewhere, Fourtou said. Otherwise they will steal too much time, energy, and effort.

How do you know the difference between people who are perpetual naysayers and those who simply disagree (and could be right)? It's subtle. When people disagree with your *ideas,* embrace them. They are your antidote to insularity. Those people may ultimately save your organization from a calamitous fate. But when people disagree with *you*—your position, authority, and level in the organization—they should seek other lines of work. When people do not respect you as the owner of your job and won't let you control your space, it's time to ease them out the door.

Ramit Varma and Jake Neuberg are cofounders of Revolution Prep, a fast-growing (up 80 percent in 2008) company that prepares students to take college and graduate school admissions tests, provides students with tutoring, and sells online services to schools. Revolution Prep employs seventy people around the country, along with seven hundred part-time teachers. In a short time, Varma and Neuberg have built a strong, common purpose culture of mostly young people who are fiercely loyal to the mission of the company and the needs of the students it serves. For most of its full-time employees, Revolution is their first job after completing college.

So how do the cofounders of this dynamic company view dissent? They embrace it when it's productive and use it to find new, creative ideas. They use dissent to solve problems and find new pathways to profits. But when dissent is the manifestation of a perpetually negative mind, they address it directly.

Varma explains, "You must be brutal and quick. When someone doesn't work out, you have to get rid of them. And you have to do it fast. If they don't uphold your values and vision, if they don't come around to your goals, they can do real damage. The biggest HR mistakes we've made were when we waited too long to fire someone because we thought that person might change." With this approach, initial turnover tends to be high. But once people have proved themselves, those who remain in their position tend to stay. Unfortunately the simple truth is that not everyone fits into every organization—even a common purpose organization. Fourtou, Varma, and Neuberg—and many other great leaders with whom I've spoken—agree. Whereas high-functioning organizations must be open to disagreements, arguments, and creative discord in an effort to fight insularity, they cannot tolerate people who are perpetually negative or can't find a way to get with the team.

And then there are the flatterers. These people put words in front of deeds and stroke egos instead of doing their jobs. For the sake of their careers, they'll say anything. You know the type.

If Dante wrote business books, he'd have reserved a special area of hell for these people. This type of person says to the CEO, "You're one of the most powerful people in the world. You should fly the corporate jet to those Washington hearings." Or, "You're the chairman and CEO. You deserve to furnish your office any way you want."

What's important for CEOs and other leaders, according to Rafael Pastor, CEO of Vistage International, a membership organization for CEOs, is that they must remember that "when you are a CEO, everyone is telling you what to do and giving you advice, not all of it good. So what leaders need to do is develop a council of people whose points of view they respect and trust and whom they can seek out for advice." Developing independent, trustworthy sources of information, judgment, and advice is often what separates the best leaders from all the others.

Common purpose must be protected like any other corporate or organizational asset. It's not less important than a brand or a patent. Rather, it is nothing less than the way people in an organization interact, which is why it must be guarded.

Chapter Three

LEADERS AT ALL LEVELS

TODAY ISN'T YESTERDAY

Why get rid of mindless hierarchy? Simon Cooper, president and chief operating officer of Ritz-Carlton, the luxury hotel chain division of the Marriott Corporation, gave one of the best reasons. He calls it "scriptless service." What does he mean by that? Luxury hotels, and most other businesses, for that matter, cater to a far more diverse group of people today than in the past. As a result, the types of requests Ritz-Carlton employees receive from their guests have changed. Twenty years ago, most of its properties were in the United States and catered largely to upper-level business travelers who were predominantly white, male, and traveling either alone or with a group of colleagues. This rather homogeneous group had needs that were relatively easy anticipate.

Today an upscale hotel chain like Ritz-Carlton—with many different types of properties, from hotels, to condominiums, to upscale time-shares—still serves its original client group, but it must also provide flawless luxury service to families, international travelers, and a far more diverse set of guests. In addition, there are now more Ritz-Carlton properties outside the United States than inside it. It must provide the same high levels of service in places as

Scriptless Service

- Today's environment is diverse along a number of dimensions: people, situations, competition, and the economic and regulatory environment.
- Diversity means that problem-solving scripts or manuals no longer work.
- Individuals operating in organizations have to think for themselves based on an understanding of the company's vision, mission, and brand, which requires leadership at all levels.
- At the Ritz-Carlton, everyone is a leader when it comes to creating the best possible experience for guests.

different as London, Beijing, Moscow, Doha, Bangalore, New York, and Berlin. Anyone can sell a bed for the night. What an upscale hotel chain like Ritz-Carlton must sell is an experience sufficient to justify a premium price. It also must sell a menu of options—spa treatments, health clubs, different types of dining, wine bars, and so on—to squeeze as much revenue as possible from each location.

To fulfill the needs of a more diverse group of guests, hotels must make certain that employees operate without having to read from a script that lays out a limited number of preselected solutions to a narrow set of guest requests. Cooper and his senior management team also understand that if a Ritz-Carlton employee has to call someone higher in the hierarchy to obtain permission to do something special for a guest, it will take time and ultimately become frustrating for the guest. They also understand that calling someone who is not with the guest leads to poor outcomes. And what can you say on the phone in front of the guest, anyway? "The dude is right here standing in front of me and acting hostile and like a real jerk"?

I don't think so.

Whereas checklists of choices might have worked decades ago when the hotel company's guests were much more homogeneous, it does not work in a multicultural, multilingual, multiservice, multinational world. To fulfill the needs of its guests, Ritz-Carlton employees—all of them—must become leaders, and at every level.

Why do I say "leaders" and not simply "good employees," or, "team members," or "associates"? Because leadership is about making decisions and rallying resources, human and otherwise, in pursuit of an objective. It means sticking your neck out and taking risks on behalf of the organization.

If you are a Simon Cooper–level leader at Ritz-Carlton, that means making decisions about the chain's future and mobilizing thousands of people around the world, along with millions of dollars, to achieve your ends. It means bringing people together to write a strategy and making certain its execution happens flawlessly. It means putting your arm around a disheartened hotel manager and bringing him or her back to peak performance. It means taking your largest customers out for a round of golf.

If you are a chambermaid-level leader, it means deciding whether to put more towels or bottles of shampoo in the bathroom after noticing how a guest used the previous ones.

If you are a front desk agent, it means deciding to upgrade a regular guest who just spent nine hours on what should have been a three-hour flight.

And if you are a maitre d', it means deciding to take drink orders yourself when the wait staff is overloaded.

Employees deciding on their own how to make guests happy is what Cooper means by *scriptless service*. They must make decisions on their own, on the spot, using their own judgment, and with the sense of confidence that comes from owning their own jobs. That's real leadership.

And it's not just businesses that require scriptless service.

A Scriptless Military

Even the U.S. military, with its conservative rank structure, is attempting to push leadership and decision making downward through the organization. Navy Vice Admiral Arthur Cebrowski, head of force transformation at the Pentagon until his death in 2005, argued that thanks to technology, U.S. combat troops have become frontline knowledge workers, not brain-dead grunts. Cebrowski was one of the most intelligent and able officers that I have ever met. His ability to look at technology, systems, and people and to conceptualize how they all needed to work together was second to none. His thoughts have great applicability to the world of business and strategy.

Shortly before his death, Cebrowski told me that small groups of soldiers were no longer in the field to carry out search-and-destroy missions. Rather, they were there to conduct "seek-and-discover" operations. This is not merely semantics. If a group of soldiers found an enemy position, a soldier's job has been transformed from simply reacting to deciding on the spot what to do from a broad menu of options. What has changed is that soldiers in the field are now linked to the entire military and all of its vast resources.

Knowledge worker soldiers, when finding an enemy, can do anything from take care of the threat on their own, ask for intelligence from drone aircraft or satellites, call for reinforcements, request air strikes or cruise missile attacks, or ask for bombing runs. There are many other options as well.

The point is that soldiers, like hotel workers or any other knowledge and service workers, are confronted with far more diversity in their day-to-day jobs along with a more diverse set of problems and a more diverse set of solutions. To make the right decisions quickly, when faced with so many choices, requires a deep understanding of each organization's mission and methods and what it stands for. It requires knowing values and its purpose.

In quickly changing and dangerous situations, rather than have a faraway group of superiors plot each soldier's movements, Cebrowski envisioned a future in which frontline soldiers, no matter their rank, would operate as leaders—exchanging information, requesting services, and offering assessments.

People working in organizations everywhere increasingly are being asked to act like leaders. They are being asked to make decisions on the spot that can have large-scale implications. To make decisions like these requires a deep understanding of the organization's common purpose.

How to Make Decisions

What criteria do people need to make those decisions?

Just as Harvey Golub stated earlier in this book, people must make decisions based on an understanding of the brand, or organizational identity, and the types of experiences associated with the brand or identity. Golub was an accomplished baker and often brought in homemade bread to the people who worked for him. But he was also a shrewd business leader. When he took over American Express, it was quite a troubled company. When he turned it over to Kenneth Chenault, its current chairman and CEO, it was once again a world leader. Golub's secret, he said, was that he understood that business is about people.

This type of direct, internal knowledge is needed to establish a sense of common purpose. But leaders also must make decisions based on their own experience, how they see other leaders act inside the organization, and because they understand, know, and have internalized the organization's common purpose.

Decision making based on common purpose applies to leaders at all levels. Everyone, from the CEO down, must be trained and educated to understand what their organization stands for, why it is different from others, and what the experiences that it delivers are like.

Let's look at another extremely successful hotel operator and how he transfers a sense of common purpose throughout the organization he leads. Steve Wynn, chairman of the multibillion dollar Wynn Resorts in Las Vegas and Macao, is a consummate hotelier, showman, casino operator, and real estate operator. One day he explained something interesting about how he is able to get his employees to transfer what they know to one another so that each of them really grasps the essence of the Wynn Resorts experience.

Wynn said that in his world, where many employees work for minimum wages plus tips, he understood that if they could tell stories to one another about how they went all out for a guest, they would communicate the essence of the brand. He said that if employees working at his resorts could talk about what he called their "heroism in the service of their guests," they would grasp what a Wynn Resorts experience should mean. By doing that they would create and communicate their common purpose.

So Wynn's developers built an internal web site where the company's employees could tell stories about what they did to make guests happy. The company then trained its employees to use it.

Leadership at Wynn Resorts

- Individuals working at the Wynn tell stories about the heroics they did to help guests.
- The Wynn maintains the technology so each employee can tell his or her story.
- People write up their "heroics" on behalf of the hotel and its guests and are recognized for it.
- These heroics become exploits that other employees model, which builds the culture by emphasizing that everyone working at the hotel is a leader, even if they are paid only minimum wage plus tips.

People write up their "heroics" on behalf of the hotel and its guests and are recognized for it. One story, which Wynn related, was about a bellmen's heroic efforts. The story began in an ordinary way when he carried an elderly guest's bags up to her room.

The guest, who had flown to Las Vegas from Los Angeles and was traveling alone, realized as she walked into the room that she had forgotten her pills. The bellman saw how anxious the woman had suddenly become when she realized she had forgotten her medicine. And since fun and entertainment—not anxiety and sickness!—are the purposes of a visit to a Wynn Resort, the bellman decided to act.

"Don't worry," the bellman told the woman. "I want you to have a good time, so I'll get your pills."

The bellman wrote down the woman's address in Los Angeles, and at the end of his shift and on his own initiative, he changed his clothes, went down to the employee parking lot, and got into his car. He filled the tank with gas and proceeded to drive four and half hours through the desert to the Los Angeles suburb where the woman lived. He knocked on the door to the house and was let inside by the woman's son, who handed the bellman the bottle of pills.

The bellman then climbed back into his car and drove another four and half hours to Las Vegas. When he arrived, he put on his uniform, rode the elevator to the guest's floor, and delivered the pills to an astonished, delighted, and relieved woman.

When he was finished, he went to the employee lounge and posted his story on the Web site so other people could learn from his actions on behalf of a guest. Wynn said the site now has hundreds of stories describing employees performing such acts. And, most important, Wynn himself reads them: bellmen, clerks, waiters, and maintenance people know the company's founder is seeing and thinking about their stories of heroism at work.

Can there be any doubt about the bellman's leadership skills? Is there any ambiguity about what "common purpose" means for people working at a Wynn Resort property? And after reading the account, would anyone doubt what the brand or the company stands for? And what about the fact that he was so conscientious about his job that he raced hundreds of miles at his own expense? The culture at Wynn rewards heroes with respect and gratitude, and here was an individual who in his own way proved his worth. And by doing it all on his own time, he demonstrated that his commitment to the organization was 24/7, not just when he was on the clock.

It Starts at the Top

In some organizations, when the official day is over at five or six o'clock or later, the cars are lined up at the exits from the parking lot like jetliners on the runway. Everyone is fleeing the building as soon as they can. And yet there are common purpose organizations where people really put in that extra effort, like the bellman at the Wynn did. How does that happen?

The starting point in a common purpose organization is always the top leader. At Wynn Resorts, everyone knows that Steve Wynn, the chairman and CEO, cares so much about his properties that he lived in a suite at the Wynn Resort in Las Vegas. People also understand that he cares about the hotels and the development of Las Vegas. And because he's the founder of the company, there is admiration, rather than jealousy, about his wealth. People understand that without Wynn and his entrepreneurial instincts, they would be out of work.

In my own experience, I have seen how great leaders put their stamp on an organization and how that stamp is replicated throughout the organization. At Continental Airlines, an airline once viewed as the worst in the industry, Gordon Bethune turned around the company with simple ideas everyone could understand and with a high level of integrity.

The first time I met Bethune was shortly after he became CEO in 1995. He was famous at Continental for inviting people into his office for a pizza lunch to discuss ways to make the airline better. He got great ideas in this way, but he also was able to change the culture of the airline through the strength of his personality. At Continental, people used to say, "Gordon's the real thing." His authenticity counted for a lot—so much so that after he retired in 2004, the company's performance deteriorated, a powerful indicator of the importance of leadership and a reminder that each generation of leaders must do its part to maintain its lead.

Bethune, who began his career as an aircraft mechanic, understood that after safety, the most important metric in the industry was an airline's on-time performance. By focusing on this single metric, everyone's behavior changed. "It's pretty simple," he told me. "You focus on the wrong things, you get the wrong result." To succeed, Bethune said, your customer's definition of success has to be your own definition of success. And since customers valued on-time performance above everything else, even price, he made it the measure of the company's success.

But you can't just pick a metric and expect to create a sense of common purpose around it. You need to communicate the importance throughout the organization in a way everyone understands. So beginning when he took over as CEO, Bethune decided to send every employee a check each time the airline was number one in on-time performance.

"We had payroll cut a separate check, not part of the paycheck, and no direct deposits. The checks were sent home. And I had the FICA and income taxes paid. These checks weren't big—fifty-five dollars. And on the memo it said, 'Thank you for helping us be on time.'" Since everyone got the check at home, everyone they lived with knew about their success. This check amplified Bethune's vision and transmitted it throughout the company. If someone used the money to go out for dinner, chances are that person told colleagues. If someone used it to make a credit card payment, chances are the person talked about that too. Bethune created not just a metric, but a way of communicating about an important element vital to creating common purpose throughout the airline. Everyone's success was rewarded when the airline succeeded: pilots, flight attendants, agents, mechanics, baggage handlers, and everyone else. As Bethune described it, the checks reminded people that they had a goal and then rewarded them when they achieved it. Rewarding the entire company without exception when the airline succeeded made everyone not only realize but feel "we're in it together," Bethune said.

A lot followed from creating a single metric that helped people coalesce around a common purpose. Flight attendants, pilots, cleaners, and everyone else did their part. People shared experiences about what they did to make certain that planes departed on time. Bethune installed an 800 number so employees could call and get help if there was a problem. "If there was always a truck in the way in the parking lot that caused delays, you'd call it in," he said. So the organization itself began to reform itself around this common purpose goal. There were daily news reports, online bulletin boards, and voice mails that employees could listen to regarding changes in the way bags were handled or planes were maintained. The point is that Bethune's choice of this single, extremely important metric led to a vast array of changes throughout the entire company. Not only that, but it changed who got promoted and who was left behind.

By choosing to use a single metric and to reward everyone, instead of creating competition between different groups inside the airline or between different crews based in different cities, Bethune was able to create a feeling that "we're all one team." After that, Bethune put in other programs to reinforce a feeling that everyone was on the same team, like profit sharing. But what Bethune did not do was reward individual behavior above team or airline-wide behavior. "Business is a team sport," Bethune told me. It's a "team of thousands because you can't do it on your own."

Common purpose requires common goals. It also requires communicating what's expected and providing feedback when people get it right. In the case of Wynn Resorts, feedback is a chance to tell a story. In the case of Continental Airlines, feedback comes in the form of a check. But in each case, people need to understand how close they come to the standard.

Chapter Four

Internalizing What the Organization Stands For

The Common Purpose Organization

The first thing you notice when you drive into the parking lot of FM Global's world headquarters in Johnston, Rhode Island, is that there are more cars in the lot set aside for employees with twenty-five or more years of service than in the general parking lot. That's unusual considering how frayed the bonds of loyalty have become in most organizations and how transient the workforce has become. And yet at FM Global, most employees still take the long view and expect to work at this innovative, 175-year-old property insurance company their entire careers. "Working here is like being part of a family," one FM Global employee told me. "I've been here twenty-nine years, which means I know everyone, and knowing who to ask really helps me get things done quickly." For companies, loyalty is not without its rewards.

FM Global employs about forty-five hundred people worldwide, about 40 percent of whom are engineers. It has about $5 billion in revenues and insures about $7 trillion in property in 130 countries around the world. One out of every three Fortune 1000 companies is an FM Global client. Although it is relatively small when compared to multiline and life insurance companies, FM Global leads the industry in almost every important measure. In 2009, Greenwich Associates, an independent research firm, ranked FM Global number one among its competitors in five categories:

- Overall customer service
- Underwriting expertise
- Ease of working relationship
- Claims processing responsiveness
- Willingness to pay claims

Greenwich Associates arrived at its conclusions after surveying insurance buyers at 669 large U.S. companies.

Another indication of FM Global's industry leadership is its extremely high client retention rate—95 percent in 2008—with many clients loyal for decades. Forty percent of FM Global's clients have been with the firm for twenty-five years or more. A few, like Johnson & Johnson, the big health care company, have been FM Global clients for more than a hundred years. General Electric has been a client of FM Global since Thomas A. Edison started it.

And as I observed in the FM Global parking lot, the firm has very low levels of employee turnover, with dozens of employees still working after forty years. The average FM Global employee is forty-three years old.

But perhaps most important from a business perspective, FM Global leads the industry in a measure called the combined ratio: revenue minus expenses, including expenses related to paying claims to clients who've suffered losses from calamities like fires, earthquakes, floods, tornados, and hurricanes. (The combined ratio does not include a firm's return on its invested capital, where FM Global also scores well.) The combined ratio is the gold standard by which the insurance industry measures its overall performance. In its category of property insurers, FM Global is at the top of the list.

LEADERSHIP AT THE START

FM Global got its start in 1835 during Andrew Jackson's second term in office as president of the United States. The world back then was very different from what it is today. Slavery was still in effect, women did not have the right to vote, steam power was in its infancy, oceangoing ships had sails and were made of wood, electricity was a laboratory curiosity, and the only things that flew were insects, birds, and bats, along with the occasional hot air balloon. It was a very different world. And yet despite the passage of time and all that has ensued, FM Global has remained remarkably true to its founding leader's vision and values. It has maintained its constancy and position despite 175 years of continuous change. In the course of getting to know FM Global, I met with team members from around the world at sessions in Singapore, Paris, and Las Vegas. What persuaded me that this was a very special company was the quality of the people and the strength of their commitment to each other, their clients, and their organization.

FM Global was started by Zachariah Allen, a Rhode Island textile mill operator who believed most losses were preventable. This phrase, "preventable losses," uttered by Allen so many years ago, continues to be repeated by people working in the firm—from its chairman and CEO throughout the organization and around the world.

This core principle, now 175 years old, remains in full force today. In fact, it is one of the most important organizing principles at FM Global and is fundamental to the way it conducts its business, thinks about the world, and writes policies.

The concept of what Allen called preventable losses is fundamental to the way the firm is structured and managed and to those it recruits to join the firm. It is critical to the way the firm is led. Allen's vision is the reason FM Global hires engineers instead of actuaries, something unique in the insurance industry.

Actuaries, a mainstay of the insurance industry, are highly trained individuals who uses statistics to assess risks by looking at what happened in the past. They crunch through mountains of data and build complex computer models that attempt to forecast the likelihood of a risk turning into a problem that results in a loss. Then actuaries attempt to extrapolate the financial impact of the loss, should it occur. Actuaries don't deal with specific problems—the likelihood of a warehouse in Wichita going up in flames, for example. For the most part, they deal in larger, statistically meaningful numbers—for example, the likelihood of a warehouse in Kansas, Nebraska, and Oklahoma going up in flames.

By making educated guesses about the number of fires, hurricanes, tornadoes, or earthquakes happening in a given year, actuaries help mainstream insurance companies forecast future financial losses. Using that information, insurance companies set the rates they charge their clients, determine how much cash to hold in reserve, and forecast profits. Armed with that information, an insurance company's sales force sells the company's policies.

The mainstream actuarial approach to insuring risks is an almost exclusively financial approach. It is mathematical and abstract. The customized, expert approach FM Global takes puts it in the minority-of-one category—no other insurance company uses the business model. To maintain its unique business model requires not just self-confidence, something FM Global has in spades, but also a special kind of fortitude since most organizations are in the business of copying what other businesses do.

FM Global, unlike almost all other insurance companies, does not use any actuaries. None are on its payroll. Instead, FM Global employs more than fourteen hundred university-educated engineers, many of whom go into the field and examine firsthand the factories, warehouses, hotels, office buildings, machinery, boilers, ports, ships, and other things the firm insures. FM Global's sales force is made up in large measure by its engineers, who examine a client's property and price the insurance policy based on what they find.

By going to a location with an engineer's deep knowledge, experience, and sensibilities, FM Global's takes a sharply different approach than its rivals do. And while the industry calls FM Global an insurance company, I call it an engineering firm that happens to be in the property protection business.

FM Global's approach is the same one that Zachariah Allen developed 175 years age. Rather than insuring against risk, FM Global does what it can to prevent problems. And if it fails at preventing a risk from turning into a loss, it pays its client to repair the damage and covers the interruption of the business. Pretty straightforward.

Before writing a policy, an FM Global engineer might go to a warehouse in an urban location and advise the owner to put in a sprinkler system to stop a fire, should one ever start. Or an FM Global engineer might sit down with a computer manufacturer to assess the security, safety, and risks associated with its global supply chain. Are the warehouses at the ports protected against fires? Are the truck depots secure? FM Global's engineers define their roles when working with clients in leadership terms. They help to secure a client's business, not just a client's buildings. It's an approach no actuary's study can match.

An FM Global engineer might work with a hotel developer in hurricane-prone Florida, Malaysia, or Indonesia and advise the developer with regard to the types of wind-resistant roofing materials to use or the types of windows or backup generators and pumps to install. If a client employs risk-abatement measures, FM

Global is able to charge less for its policies. In that way, an FM Global engineer becomes a leading member of the client's team.

By using engineers rather than actuaries, FM Global controls its costs and losses by stopping bad things from happening. And because it puts its money where its mind is, the firm has a sixteen-hundred-acre research campus in western Rhode Island. On the grounds of its campus, FM Global tests fire abatement equipment, designs new fire-suppression sprinklers, and researches better ways to build. Like most engineering firms, FM Global holds many patents.

LEADERSHIP AT FM GLOBAL

I am calling attention to FM Global's singular approach to its business not because this is a book about the insurance business. Far from it. Rather, my point in focusing on FM Global is to describe how common purpose leadership works in a real setting and how the vision, mission, values, and practices of common purpose leaders can be highly profitable without eroding over time.

In fact, FM Global has been a common purpose company since its inception, an attribute that imbued it with enormous staying power and resiliency. And unlike GM, for example, whose problems were observed by Peter Drucker (but ignored) as early as 1943, FM Global has struggled hard against insularity and arrogance. In fact, what I would call "self-confident humility" is a value that is deeply embedded in the FM Global culture.

FM Global has preserved its values and its founder's vision not by using hard power (to borrow a phrase that refers to diplomacy through warfare and threat). It has not used authoritarian programs of firings, harsh discipline, and tough-sounding memos. Rather, leadership has been communicated throughout the firm using soft power: techniques of building a culture where consensus matters not as a tool for stifling dissent or to slow decision making but to make certain everyone's views are heard.

This is subtle. In many organizations, even in some so-called flat organizations, decision making proceeds from the top. The top team decrees something, and the rank and file are expected to carry it out. The decree may be cheerful and even correct, but it is still a decree.

Common purpose organizations hold to the view that knowledge is developed and embedded throughout the organization, not just at the top. One business leader I admire, Minoru Makihara, who led Japan's Mitsubishi Corporation when it was the world's largest company, told me that when he made decisions, he communicated them throughout the global organization and even to affiliated companies. But he always also listened to what came back and adjusted his decisions accordingly. "I think we have to lead people by being good listeners," he said. Why did he put it that way? Because if you list who owns the company, Makihara told me, the employees would be first on the list. They would be number one not because of the stock they held but because of the time they invest in their jobs and because of what they know. Common purpose leaders understand this.

FM Global has been able to employ its approach partly because it selects people to join the firm who fit with the organization's goals and adhere to its values, mission, and practices. And it has done so by promoting into the top team a group of people who lead by example. Among the top team, there is a value placed on service, listening, coaching, self-confident humility, and accessibility. FM Global is a common purpose company not just because its chairman/CEO keeps his office door open. It is a rare company because Shivan Subramaniam, FM Global's chairman and CEO, listens to what's on people's minds. In fact, he takes every opportunity he can to listen to what FM Global's people think, even eating in the company's cafeteria and often sitting at

---

Common Purpose Leadership at FM Global

- Vision: Most losses are preventable.
- Core values: The development, application, and sharing of knowledge is the best tool to use to prevent losses.
- Mission: Savings from preventing losses should be shared among the firm's "members," the largest of whom make up the firm's board and advisory groups.
- Leadership style: Self-confident but humble; decision making distributed widely; leading by sharing the same vision, values, and mission
- Result: Long-term loyalty among customers, staff, and leadership; high levels of accountability, responsibility, and initiative; upbeat corporate culture

---

random with a group of FM Global employees. Subramaniam wants to hear what they think.

FM GLOBAL'S PRACTICAL VALUES

Allen's idea to insure only "highly protected risks" was pretty simple back in the 1800s. It might mean removing oil-soaked rags, sawdust, and textile remnants from the premises. A little later, it meant adding fire prevention equipment like sprinklers and pre-positioning firefighting equipment: ladders, hoses, water tanks, axes, buckets, and protective clothing. In the 1800s, when so many buildings were made of wood and so little plumbing was in use, fire was a constant danger. So to insure only highly protected risks meant a high level of participation from mill owners and managers in maintenance and design of the locations.

FM Global's founding leadership principles were not fluff or marketing hype. They were honest and true, and they saved lives and property. All of these elements were solid building blocks for a common purpose organization.

But there is more. In his formulation, Allen made it a requirement that companies insured by FM Global be inspected regularly to make certain their efforts were up to date. It's not that Allen didn't trust his members. He did. But he also knew that people are human and not always above cutting corners. As a result, he trusted, but he also required verification—a practice FM Global still employs.

Just as important as verifying that member companies did what they said they would do was the knowledge gained from undertaking those inspections. Some members did the minimum, but others were innovative and embraced the common purpose of FM Global's protect-against-losses cause. That meant new techniques for protecting mills and factories against risks could be transferred among the mutual's members. By doing this, Allen set up a system for transferring what would later be termed best practices. Transferring knowledge from one client to another remains an important element in FM Global's success. It is part of the mutual's common purpose core.

Since only a third of FM Global's employees are engineers, the firm teaches its other employees to think like engineers in order to achieve common purpose. It does this through well-developed training programs with dozens of offerings that includes Engineering 101, an important course that helps people see the world in similar ways. It builds bridges throughout the organization.

Other organizations use other languages to express their purpose and view the world. A number of successful organizations, such as Coca Cola and McDonald's, use the language of marketing and sales to communicate throughout the organization. Other organizations look at the world from a financial point of view, as Goldman Sachs and Credit Suisse do. Still others look at their business from a client-centric point of view. There are a number of different ways to create a worldview.

When I worked at *The New York Times,* we usually discussed issues from the point of view of what we called the "reader," an idealized person somewhere who, we imagined, was reading our stories. We tried to report, write, and edit each piece in ways that would help that reader understand. When I was the editor of the *Harvard Business Review,* we discussed our work from the vantage point of "the manager." And at PricewaterhouseCoopers, where I was a partner, everyone used the language and mind-set of accounting to discuss issues inside and outside of the firm. What was that mind-set? As one of my partners put it, "Thinking like an accountant means you are always worrying on behalf of your client that something really big and important might have slipped through the cracks. As the accountant, you have to find what that thing was." At PricewaterhouseCoopers, thinking like an accountant created a shared sense of, well, worry, but it also created a shared sense of purpose.

Embedded in a firm's language is a set of assumptions that enable people to discuss and solve problems in a kind of shorthand. These commonly held assumptions have power and help make each organization unique. They also make it difficult for one organization to copy another's business model. And they offer clues to each organization's hidden vulnerabilities.

All organizations have embedded assumptions. At Microsoft, for example, I observed that these assumptions focused on the belief that superior intelligence, combined with tenacity and aggressiveness toward the accomplishment of a goal, could solve any problem. At Microsoft, people were hired based on how smart they were and how aggressively they pursued goals. They were promoted for the same reasons. Leaders at Microsoft were often ferocious in meetings and rarely cared about feelings or even group cohesiveness. I recall several meetings at Microsoft in its early days that were strongly animated mixtures of raw intelligence and high levels of aggression. It was not uncommon for people to call each other stupid or to dismiss someone's idea with groans. The belief was that intelligence and aggression could solve any problem.

These types of embedded assumptions might have worked in Microsoft's early days, but when its objective was to capture the desktop, they did not work as the company matured. Lawsuits were brought against the company for unfair business practices, and the Justice Department nearly broke up the company. As a result, the culture was forced to change, and along with it so did the firm's faith in unbridled aggression. People hired a decade or two ago to work at the company might be passed over today for being too raw. In fact, at a recent meeting I led at Microsoft, one of the firm's leaders told the group, "I think, as a company, we need to be humble." This remark was vastly different from those made in the company's early days and shows how an organization's assumptions can change over time. Whereas Microsoft's core value regarding the need for people with high levels of intelligence has remained, it now recruits leaders from companies like IBM and consulting firms—organizations it once ridiculed as "mature," and "moribund," and "past it." Microsoft's newest recruits are smart, but they are also more group-oriented than before and a little less raw.

FM Global has evolved as well. In 1835, there were very few university-trained engineers. Instead, companies trained their own people, and some were better at it than others. Today engineering is a much more refined discipline. But while FM Global has evolved and professionalized itself, it has remained true to its original vision, mission, and values. As a result, the worldview promulgated more than a century ago remains intact at FM Global and continues to animate the firm.

Chapter Five

THE BEST LEADERS ARE PART OF THE GROUP

MODELING THE LEADERSHIP'S BEHAVIOR

I believe strongly that leadership must permeate an organization at all levels if it is to be successful. This challenges an outdated assumption about leadership that is essentially military in nature: that a leader is in command of others. And while sometimes that type of leadership is what we get, it's rarely what we need. The world is simply too complicated for a command-and-control type of leader. Perhaps it always was. The command-and-control leaders who took charge at the governmental level—Stalin, Hitler, Mao, Mussolini, Saddam Hussein—produced disastrous results. Inside organizations, command-and-control leadership—dominance—has had the same sad history. Consider Tyco under the iron hand of Dennis Kozlowski and Enron under the leadership of Jeffrey Skilling. Within these organizations, bad behavior occurred in large measure because the leaders at the top not only condoned it, they did it themselves. Even the military has largely abandoned the idea that leadership and command are synonymous, as Admiral Arthur Cebrowski and others have said.

Leadership is really about guiding, coaching, or even inspiring others to reach a goal. Sometimes a leader stands in front, sometimes to the side, sometimes even behind the people he or she is trying to help reach a goal. This approach to leadership means that it's not just the man or woman at the top who is responsible. Instead, everyone in an organization shares responsibility for reaching a goal. Sometimes, of course, the structure of the organization can get in the way of leading. At other times, people can have that effect. The point is that while great leadership is never easy, as Ronald Heifetz, a psychiatrist and leadership expert at Harvard's John F. Kennedy School of Government and others point out, now, more than ever before, it is distributed.

Without highly motivated, empowered employees such as the bellman at Wynn Resorts, an organization cannot survive for long in today's hypercompetitive, volatile, global environment. For example, as Peter Maslin, former president of Starbucks International, explained to me, most of Starbucks's really great ideas came from the field—people working in individual stores who are innovators. According to Maslin, what Starbucks and his team did was to create a system within the company to capture the ideas and innovations of these far-flung leaders and teach them to others around the world. Leadership, to Maslin, is about capturing something new, cool, and important that was done in a store in, say, Dubai and transfer that to London, Kansas City, Beijing, and elsewhere. To carry that out means ridding an organization of the idea that leadership is about commanding others to fulfill your vision in favor of recognizing that everyone in the organization can contribute to achieving the organization's greater goals while helping others do so as well.

Individuals take their cues from the way other people in the organization behave. They look to the right and left, but they also look at the top leaders of their organizations for ways to model their behavior. They look at the top team because even though modern organizations require leadership at all levels, the people at the top have the most leverage. People within organizations tend to model the behavior of the people at the top.

When the people at the top of an organization are greedy or mistrustful, it is impossible to keep that type of behavior from permeating the entire organization. Consciously or unconsciously, people working inside an organization copy behaviors that are rewarded and that they perceive are necessary to get ahead. As strange as it may seem, in some organizations, people model the personality styles of the individuals at the top.

I have seen this type of modeling take place countless times. When Bill Gates still worked at Microsoft on a day-to-day basis as founder, chairman, and CEO, I saw many people adopt his rather idiosyncratic mannerism of rocking back and forth in his seat as he listened to others speak. Some people at Microsoft even adopted Gates's way of talking, elongating their vowels and taking on a Seattle accent even if they were born and educated in London or Mumbai.

At now-defunct Lehman Brothers (once an important global financial institution), Dick Fuld, the last CEO, took home more than $500 million during his career. As a result of his example, other people in the organization felt it was not only okay but justified to take outrageous chances in order to make the kind of money Fuld did, even if they did so at the shareholders' expense.

An organization's top leaders are responsible for the fate of the organization often in ways they do not fully comprehend. They are responsible for their organizations by the actions they take but also because of the behaviors they exhibit. A leader (at any level but most certainly at the top level) cannot say, "The firm failed in spite of me." Unfortunately, it doesn't work that way. Organizations are inanimate. They are simply ways people select to organize the work they do. They do not have feelings and make no decisions. If the organization inhibits action, it is up to the human beings who work inside it to make changes.

How People View Leaders

- People watch their leaders in microscopic detail.
- Individuals working within a firm tend to copy their leaders' style.
- Leaders find that others copy their worst characteristics along with their best traits.
- Leaders must be disciplined to made certain that they exhibit only the types of behavior they want others in the company to share.

Certainly success is the business of everyone in the organization, but its top leaders are more responsible for the organization's success than are others because of the leverage they hold and the resources they have at their fingertips. They are also responsible because of the behaviors they use, which are transmitted throughout the organization and which others model. Gates's rocking back and forth in his chair may have been modeled by hundreds of his wannabe successors at Microsoft, but so was his ability to work hard, push himself intellectually, and always put the success of the firm first. And while Gates became one of the world's richest men, he shared the wealth the company created, helping several others become billionaires and hundreds of others become millionaires. Gates became wealthy, but he was never greedy. In fact, he became massively philanthropic. And as his philanthropic activities grew, others at Microsoft modeled that behavior too.

I have seen organizations in which people drive the same car as the CEO, play the same sports, use the same golf clubs, and wear the same brands of clothes. At one global company I know, members of the top team, as well as others, lived in the same neighborhood, sent their kids to the same private schools, and went to the same church, even if it was a different religion from the one they belonged to prior to joining the organization.

What Fuld, Gates, and others show is that no senior leader in an organization, *especially the CEO,* can ever be invisible, no matter how insulated. People will model the behaviors of the people at the top.

One global organization I know was led by a charismatic, hyperactive, highly effective CEO who also happened to be a womanizer with a string of infidelities involving coworkers and several failed marriages. Strangely, people working with this particular CEO began modeling his behavior. People even quipped that getting divorced and having affairs was part of the corporate culture.

Psychologists, anthropologists, and neuroscientists might be able to explain why people in organizations model their leaders' behavior. In fact, according to neurologists like V. S. Ramachandran, at the University of California, San Diego, our brains have a set of neurons, called mirror neurons, that are specialized so we can observe and copy the behavior of others. These neurons are used in part for learning languages, but they are also used to copy behaviors. These neurons don't switch off because we work in big, modern organizations, drive cars, and ride in planes. They are always there, always on, always functioning. This means that individuals inside organizations watch and copy the people at the top. In fact, they watch them extremely carefully.

What does all this tell you? Leadership is not just about what you do. It is also about who you are. Character not only counts; it is an important force for change.

CASE STUDY: FM GLOBAL

Over the past thirty years, I have met, interviewed, and worked with many leaders running Fortune 500 companies and leaders in government and nonprofits. I would have said, "I had the pleasure of meeting," but unfortunately it wasn't quite that way. Too many of the leaders I met were simply not very good at what they did. Too few had the courage it takes to be great, and too many thought that becoming CEO was their birthright. But as Bruce Pasternack, a consultant and investor, wrote in *The Centerless Corporation,* becoming a CEO is "a promotion, not a coronation."

One leader who gets it is Shivan Subramaniam, chairman and CEO of FM Global. Subramaniam and his top team of leaders are among the finest and most able group of leaders I have met. They are also common purpose leaders, which is to say they are at the forefront of how leadership is evolving.

Modeling the Top Team

At FM Global, as in all other organizations, people throughout the company model the behavior exhibited by the top team. But whereas most leaders are oblivious to this fact, FM Global's leaders understand it and work with it.

Subramaniam, who was born in India, exhibits all of the characteristics of self-confident humility. "Given my position at the firm, there's one thing I recognize. Despite what I might think or feel about myself, people are watching me," he said. "That makes it very important for me to be careful about how I treat other people. That's because I'm always amazed at how many people know about what I do. So I'm always very careful about my behavior."

Subramaniam said that being aware that people are watching you means treating everyone with respect: "You cannot treat yourself any differently from the way you treat others."

Subramaniam is respected at FM Global for the type of person he is and for the qualities he displays. As a leader, he is known to be smart, thoughtful, and tough-minded. But he is also modest. Subramaniam mixes easily with other employees of the organization in the cafeteria and elsewhere. He does that because while he may be chairman and CEO, he also considers himself an FM Global employee.

Subramaniam subjects himself to the same rules and regulations as everyone else, and he does it with sincerity and without pretense. For example, when I met him at FM Global's headquarters in Rhode Island, I was told that he would be a little late. The reason I was given was that he had meetings in San Francisco that had gone long. As a consequence, he took a commercial red-eye flight from San Francisco to Boston and then traveled by car to Rhode Island so he wouldn't have to miss our meeting.

A chairman and CEO traveling commercial? On a red-eye flight? He did it, I was told by several people within the company who work closely with him, because Subramaniam made a commitment to see me and he "never takes his commitments lightly."

As everyone knows, red-eye flights, which leave the West Coast around 10:00 P.M. and arrive on the East Coast at 5:00 A.M. or 6:00 A.M., due to the time difference, are never pleasant. They mean at best a fitful night with only a couple of hours of sleep.

While it may be a good and cheap way to fly across the country if you are a student, backpacker, young professional, or running a start-up, it's exceedingly rare to find the CEO of a Fortune 1000 company curled up on board such a flight. In fact, I know of only one CEO who would take such a flight: Subramaniam.

"Several times," Subramaniam told me, "my board said, 'Why don't you get a private jet?' FM Global is of the size that it can very easily do it, and there are obvious conveniences and efficiencies. But I told the board that I felt it would send a terrible message throughout the company if we bought a private jet. First, it's so expensive. In fact, I don't know how anybody justifies owning a jet on the basis of cost alone. But even if it made sense financially, it just doesn't set the right tone. If you treat yourself a little differently from others, how do you expect everybody else to behave? What message does that send?"

Leadership Rules According to FM Global

- People always watch the people at the top. You can't change that, but you can use it to the organization's advantage.
- Leaders cannot treat themselves differently from other people in the organization.
- True leaders know when to let other people lead, even if doing so puts them out of their comfort zone.
- Leaders need to have character, but they also must be able to perform.
- Great leaders move quickly when necessary, but they allow themselves enough time to make the right decision.

One of the ways Subramaniam leads is by recognizing that though he may be chairman and CEO of a high-performance, highly profitable company, that gives him no dictatorial powers. "We have a rule that says executives at a certain level in the company can fly business class but only if it's a flight of two hours or more. I observe that rule myself," he said. "I do it because if we're insisting that that's a rule we have for our senior people, then there shouldn't be another rule for me. It doesn't make sense. I think it's very important that leaders don't treat themselves differently from how they treat others."

What type of results does FM Global get from the way Subramaniam leads? People within the company model his behavior. One senior manager responsible for FM Global's client meetings globally said she qualifies for business class when she flies but rarely uses it: "I just try to save money for the firm." This long-serving FM Global veteran consciously downgrades her air travel and even her hotel accommodations as a point of pride. "Saving money for the firm is just the right thing to do," she said. "And if Shivan [Subramaniam] can do it, why can't I?"

In addition, as Subramaniam pointed out, great leaders have to get out of their comfort zones. Although a leader might love to analyze spreadsheets, as Subramaniam does, he or she has to resist the temptation of doing it if someone else is better suited to the task. That means leaders are not always doing the things they love to do. For Subramaniam, who is highly analytical by nature, that means backing off when it's time to pore over the intricacies of a spreadsheet or financial model so that others can learn and develop the skills and confidence they need.

Leader as Coach?

For some people, Subramaniam might be thought of as the leader as coach. But I think that's far too narrow a description of how he views his role and performs his leadership tasks. And while it's true that he is a coach, he is much more: "I think the focus of our management teams is that we all help people to get to the right place. Our style is not to tell people what to do. Instead, we're interested in helping them think through what they have to do to make their own decisions. So we don't spend a lot of time telling people what to do. Instead, we talk about the issues. Each person who reports to me has leadership responsibilities of their own. It's not up to me to undermine them. Besides, since I have eight direct reports, I can't direct them and tell them what to do. As a result, people don't come to me for a decision. They come to discuss things."

But while these comments indicate that Subramaniam pays enormous attention to making certain he does not undermine others in the company and imposes discipline on himself to tamp down his ego and move himself out of his comfort zone, he also provides the firm with its vision and mission and holds people accountable for their results. In that way, Subramaniam is more

Shivan Subramaniam's Style of Leadership

- Discipline your ego. You can't do only things you love.
- Step outside your comfort zone. Others need to take on significant roles.
- Guide, advise, and recommend. Don't direct behavior or decide for others what they should do, or you'll lose your best people.
- Create the vision, make certain everyone's on the mission, and hold people accountable.
- Mix with everyone in the company, and never create barriers.

like a ship's captain who works with the board to find a direction, divides the work among his direct reports, and ensures that no matter what happens, the ship stays on course.

Chapter Six

CULTIVATING CURIOSITY, NOT COMPLACENCY

In some of the business literature, a team that has little turnover is considered a negative. How, these authors ask, can you keep individuals sharp and bring in new ideas if the people you work with today are the same people you worked with yesterday? But Subramaniam and others disagree. Companies are complicated and very global. They have processes and even products that are difficult to master. There are intricacies that need to be followed and subtle danger signs that need to be observed.

I once had an off-the-record lunch with the chairman and CEO of one of the world's largest companies. It was a successful company that owned many brands and had offices and manufacturing plants around the world. The CEO was a venerated business leader who had won awards; he spent a good deal of his money on philanthropy and advocated to his staff that they do the same.

But when I asked him how he keeps track of a company with more than 100,000 employees and a myriad of processes, procedures, R&D centers, customers, and locations, he looked at me and confessed, "I really don't know how the company works anymore."

Then this highly confident CEO explained that the bane of his existence had been the company's turnover at all levels. Because his company was such a strong competitor, with world-renowned training, other companies raided his employee base for talent. And while he had come up through the ranks, everyone in his "class" of budding executives who started with him years before had gone on to work elsewhere. His company had made the investment in them, but other companies reaped the rewards. Even more pertinent, each time an executive left, a knowledge gap was created. Those gaps were difficult and expensive to fill.

"You know what the friends I grew up with in this company are doing? They're working at Microsoft and IBM and Ford and GE, and they're in private equity and venture capital, and a couple are on Wall Street. They started with me, we trained them, and then they left. You know how expensive that is? And now I'm constantly having to meet new colleagues around the world. They are people of great talent but little experience in our world. We're good, but we're so frequently raided for our talent that we keep losing our best people. It's an extremely expensive problem to have, and it affects performance."

While the introduction of new talent into a company can be highly beneficial from the point of view of a cross-fertilization of ideas, each time you lose a seasoned executive, you lose knowledge, know-how, and an understanding of what might be called "go to"— knowing whom to go to in order to get something done.

Bob Joy, the legendary head of talent management (call it Global HR, if you must) at Colgate-Palmolive, saw the problem of losing highly talented individuals as one of the most important problems his company faced. Together with his CEO, the equally legendary but now retired Ruben Marks, Joy developed a system for rating individuals by whether they are high-potential, high-performance people. If one of these individuals declares his or her intentions to leave the company, the CEO must be notified within twenty-four hours of the individual's decision to leave and a counteroffer made within twenty-four hours after that.

Notify the CEO when a high-potential, high-performing person is about to leave the company anywhere in the world? You've got to be kidding! Doesn't the CEO have anything better to do? No. And not if he wants the company's vital knowledge and "go to" to remain in the firm.

"From very early on, I felt the key for us at Colgate was to focus on having the best talent. The distinction that I may have made, versus some of my peers, was that I really believed that you had to have the best talent globally. I also strongly believed that you couldn't afford to lose that talent at any level in the organization," Joy told me for a project called Creating Value Through People.

KEEPING AND CELEBRATING LEADERS

Keeping leaders from going elsewhere is not an easy task. To do that, they have to feel that they are wanted, needed, and constantly challenged. They also need to be recognized, says Joy. At Colgate, he designed a program to bring twenty-five to thirty of the company's high-potential, high-performing leaders to the company's New York headquarters, no matter where they might be based.

The program was a highly structured experience: an Outward Bound experience over a weekend, followed by five days of exposure to every part of the company on a global basis. People were brought in from around the world to interact with these high-performing, high-potential leaders. During their time in New York, they would meet and spend time with every senior manager in the company and every functional leader. Finally, the group was given a project to work on, and they would then present that work to the chairman/CEO and the company's senior leadership. At the end of the week, the chairman/CEO would host a dinner for the group. As Joy said, at the end of the program, which lasted a little over a week, the group was on cloud nine. "Talk about feeling special."

How to Retain Leaders

- Identify them early, and make sure they know it.
- Celebrate their accomplishments.
- Educate them about the organization and its capabilities.
- Give them access to the team at the top.
- Respond quickly with a counteroffer if they plan to leave.
- Reward them with new challenges, not just with more money.

An organization's leaders at all levels are its rock stars. But it's not enough to tell them that or even pay them well in appreciation. They also need to be celebrated for what they add to the organization's overall endeavor. At Wynn Resorts, a bellman can be celebrated for his accomplishments in taking care of a guest. He can post his story on the internal Web site and become a hero. At Colgate-Palmolive, the company's next generation of leaders are celebrating in ways that integrate them more closely into the firm—meetings with people from around the world and presentations for the top executives followed by dinner with the CEO. These are perks given to people with talent whose impact will reverberate around the organization.

Organizations are really nothing more than ways people have devised so that they can accomplish goals larger than an individual can pursue on his or her own. Even so, people often lose sight of the fact that the individuals working in the organization are the ones who actually accomplish goals. An IBM or Xerox or Toyota can accomplish nothing without a talented group of people working side-by-side. These individuals must be free to pursue their purpose within the organization; they must feel valued and feel that they own their job. At Colgate, people feel that way. They are celebrated as new leaders not just because they are talented but because they contribute to the common purpose of the organization. And because of visionary leaders like Bob Joy, the structure of the company has been shaped so that it enhances an individual's chances for success.

The organization at Colgate, which is built to alert the CEO when a high-potential or high-performing individual intends to leave the company, is unusual. And yet it recognizes what so many people know but do nothing about: when good people—leaders— leave an organization, they create gaps. These gaps are difficult and expensive to repair, which is why great companies place a premium on length of service.

LONGEVITY VERSUS HOMOGENEOUSNESS

At FM Global, the combined service length of the four people at the top is almost as long as the age of the company. Shivan Subramaniam jokes, "I've known some of the people on the team longer than I've known my wife."

Having a top team of leaders where there is trust and an accurate assessment of each individual's strengths and weaknesses is important. In research I conducted for a project on start-ups, I discovered that the chances of a company's success are increased by as much as 30 percent when the founders of a company have worked together in the past. This often means that those leaders who have worked together at the top for a long time have similar mental maps, similar ways of thinking, and similar ways of assessing risks and opportunities. It also means that the team at the top is homogeneous even though its members' personal backgrounds might be diverse.

A homogeneous group of leaders can function powerfully since there is little need to translate information to accommodate different points of view. They understand things the same way and are capable of moving swiftly. But a group that is homogeneous also can have blind spots. In both instances, the key to making a group of leaders work is trust. Leaders who have all been trained the same way can be open with one another, and they can voice their fears and doubts. And if they are all bound in common purpose, they have very little to hide. Each team member's agenda will be open and transparent. Each leader's personal objectives will be in plain view.

"There are different ways of leadership," offers Ruud H. Bosman, vice chairman of FM Global. "There are the ways you lead at Microsoft or at a quickly developing organization. That's one way. But we're leading a relatively stable organization, which is very different. If you take those two starting points, then I think our leadership challenge is, 'How do we maximize the upside of a very stable foundation?' We have a great platform, which, obviously, we can screw up. But what do we have to do to build on what we developed? That's a very different challenge from a young company that's interested just in staying in business."

So how does FM Global maximize the upside on a business platform where the first brick was laid in 1835? "We're an insurance company, and that's why people call us," Bosman said. According to Bosman, the first element with regard to leadership is not the individual. Rather, it is working out what he calls the organization's strategy, its common purpose. This was very evident, Bosman said, after the merger of the five related companies that were brought together to form FM Global in 1999. Once the merger went through, communicating the new firm's strategic goals, visions, and mission was critically important. Bosman, who led the process, said that was done in a "very deliberate and thorough manner. We did not want to get involved in lengthy discussions and complex explanations of who we were and where we were going, what our targets were, how we judge success, how we needed to behave in the marketplace. We wanted some very simple statements of purpose and objectives. We wanted to almost force ourselves to make it easy to communicate. I felt—and I still feel—that a lot of companies make business planning and strategy setting much too complicated. It's my view that if you are aiming for success, you'd better be able to articulate your

plans and goals very concisely instead of with twenty-five-page plans."
In other words, bringing everyone onboard with an organization's
common purpose goals means getting people to focus.

The benefits that arise from the ability to focus are profound.
"Now," Bosman explained, "when the leadership team comes
together to discuss something, our dialogue starts with a very clear
understanding of the company's purpose and goals. And that
extends throughout the company. I don't think anybody here at
FM Global is in doubt about what our business plan is about. In
addition, at this point in time, it would really surprise me if there was
any debate about that plan and our goals."

So how does FM Global make certain that everyone stays in the
loop?

"Every year," Bosman said, "we publish a little book. In it, we
lay out the year's key strategic goals. Then Shivan, Jon, Tom, and I
[the four members of FM Global's leadership team] go around the
world to every office and spend half a day with everybody making
sure they understand what's in the book and understand our goals.
We make it fun too. But it's a continuing exercise aimed at
communicating throughout the organization in a disciplined way
what we're trying to achieve. We engage the entire company in this
exercise around our purpose."

Keeping everybody informed is vital to the way FM Global
does business. The idea is that if the company is going to allow
people to make decisions, then they better know what is going on in
the company. This approach has been vital to the company's success
and also to the way it operated during the 1999 merger.

Three FM Global executives were taking an executive education course at Wharton Business School, along with twenty or so
people from other companies. When the professor asked if anyone
had been through a merger, all hands were raised. But when he asked
who had been through a successful merger, the only people to raise
their hands were those from FM Global.

"So we talked it through," said Thomas A. Lawson, FM Global's executive vice president for North and South American insurance operations. "And the professor put on the blackboard all the reasons that mergers fail—which we don't have. He said the reasons for failure have to do with issues like the need for a common language, common purpose, and a quick, effective, and efficient way to set directions—all the things we do. And it kind of occurred to those of us from FM Global that this is just how we live and the rest of the class was amazed. They were amazed, for example, that we could make a decision in an executive management meeting on Monday and see it being implemented in the field by Friday."

When I asked Lawson how FM Global could move so smoothly and efficiently from decision to action, he explained: "At FM Global, for the most part, decisions are made by people who live them. We don't go outside to hire managers. All our managers start here, and the bulk of them are in the engineering pool, except for people like our general counsel or our information technology people. So because of the common language of engineering, everyone's making decisions based on the same foundation. Our people all grew up either inspecting facilities or doing risk assessments or underwriting business or selling business, so they've all got this deep, common knowledge of the business, and that translates into how we make decisions.

"In addition," Lawson continued, "We have a very simple structure. There's not a long distance between the executive group and the people who are doing the work. And we don't have a lot of second-guessing. We all start from the same premise that the majority of losses are preventable." In addition, he explained, because of the deep pool of common knowledge and shared language, FM Global is confident about letting each person own his or her job. In so doing, rather than needing lots of hierarchy, FM Global allows decisions to be made by the people closest to them. "We have engineers with five years of experience, and we turn around and let them make decisions, and we put $1 billion of capacity behind their decisions. We do this because we know their decisions are technically sound engineering decisions. We make big bets based on these engineering assessments. That drives our entire risk assessment process."

One reason that FM Global is able to develop and maintain its sense of common purpose is the way people are paid. Subramaniam is well paid, but not four hundred times the salary of the average rank-and-file employee, which is the case at many American companies. "We're paid in the ninety-fifth percentile," Lawson said. "We're not underpaid or overpaid. But the difference is that all employees share in the success of the company, from the lowest person in the food chain all the way up. That's how everyone is incented, although there are some variations in the plan. When the company does well, we all do well. It's all based on our combined ratio, which is the money spent on losses and expenses versus the money taken in. That helps everyone focus on how to make us more profitable. It involves everyone. It makes everyone think, 'Hey, how can I get a cheaper deal on pens or paper that will help our combined ratio?' The combined ratio is easy to understand, and everybody gets it. It doesn't matter if it's a research scientist, engineer, or secretary. Everyone gets it."

FM Global has also devised a program it calls "off-boarding." It is put into practice when the firm loses a client. The idea is to document and understand why the relationship went bad, what happened, and to try to end the business relationship without animosity. "We don't want any terrorists out there," Hall said. "So we take the end of a relationship very seriously and try to end on a basis of goodwill."

EMPLOYMENT LONGEVITY

Employment longevity in a world of short-term thinking and loyalty-free employment gives a company like FM Global a powerful advantage over its rival, according to Subramaniam. The value to the organization of a team that has worked together during economic downturns and come through them successfully cannot be underestimated, he believes. In the case of FM Global, working together has led to something of a shorthand, where the top team knows each other so well they can communicate in rapid-fire sound bites.

"I think what has also helped us enormously is that we haven't had much turnover at the senior-most level of the company," Subramaniam said. "We have had a lot of stability. Because we've all worked together for a long time, we don't spend a lot of time telling people what to do. Instead, we spend time trying to talk about the issues and try to come to some kind of consensus."

How closely does the top team of leaders work together and understand each other's views?

"The way I look at it," Subramaniam said, "if I got hit by a bus, I am 100 percent confident Ruud [Bosman] could step in comfortably without missing a beat. The organization wouldn't see any change. Or if the two of us went down in a plane crash somewhere, then Tom [Lawson] or John [Hall] could step in, and people wouldn't notice that much difference. It would be fairly smooth and flawless, which is the key to any kind of transition."

Contrast that with McDonald's. In 2004, its CEO, James Cantalupo, died unexpectedly of a heart attack. Cantalupo was replaced by Charlie Bell, who was diagnosed with cancer a month after taking Cantalupo's place. He passed away a year later from cancer, leaving the company in disarray and causing it to rethink how it staffs, manages, and plans. "After that, we decided each senior job needed to have at least two people who could succeed an incumbent," Jan Fields, the chief operating officer, told me.

Having bench strength is one thing, but having bench strength where each member of the team has worked together and respects one another is another thing. "The funny thing is, we not only work together really well, we also like each other," said Lawson. "Respecting each other, like we do, is important."

COMMON PURPOSE AT THE TOP

The way Subramaniam views leadership is illustrative of how common purpose works in action. First, the top team really is a team. And rather than dictating to them his views or asking each team member to carry out a task, the top team is highly collaborative. They share the same goals for the company, uphold the same vision for its future, and genuinely want to ensure that the company succeeds. And while most of them have received at least one tempting call from a recruiter, they have remained at FM Global for reasons other than money.

Operationally, Subramaniam, as chairman and CEO, is the tie breaker if it comes to that. But he rarely invokes that role. Instead, Subramaniam sees himself as another member of the team—neither special nor privileged.

"I'm not quite sure any one of us specifically wants to be seen as the person who unilaterally sets the direction," Subramaniam told me. "Instead, I think the focus is on the fact that our jobs are to help people get to the right place. So if I had to characterize either Ruud [Bosman] or Tom [Lawson] or Jon [Hall], or even my own leadership style, I don't think it is one where we're inclined to tell people what to do. Instead our job as leaders is to help people get to the right place on their own and help them think through the important things." Other members of FM Global's senior management team told me the same thing in almost the same way. And rather than indicating some form of brainwashing, or putting FM Global into the category of a cult, what it shows is how deeply the organization is committed to a common purpose sense of leadership style in which individuals are respected and their views are not only listened to but heard.

The style of leadership that FM Global's top team exhibits is very rare. In my own experience, working with several dozens of companies for almost thirty years, I have never seen an organization where there is so much genuine respect for individuals. I have also only rarely glimpsed organizations where individuals inside companies are given the kind of authority to act that FM Global confers on its people.

But even in high-performing companies where people of a single discipline dominate, it is rare to see leaders at the highest level who truly trust other leaders who operate below them in the hierarchy.

I have often felt that a true common purpose organization would require very little management in the traditional sense of the word, where people at the top make a decision that cascades through the organization, and others act on those decisions with limited decision-making authority. Even in flat organizations, where people closest to the customer decide, a lot of second-guessing goes on when the decisions required are nuanced. But until I came in contact with FM Global, with the exception of Google, I had rarely observed a company with a relatively flat hierarchy, where so much is decided by the people closest to the client and so little second-guessing occurs.

It is not that flat organizations—scriptless organizations, if you will—simply devolve power to people closest to the customer. They also authorize people close to the customer to refrain from making a decision until they get some advice when it is needed. And in a way, the essence of flat is not when a big customer's concern escalates up for Subramaniam to decide. The essence of flat is when an engineer with five years of experience feels free enough, secure enough, and respected enough to call an engineer with fifteen years of experience to ask for help.

But there is a caveat: if you work in a common purpose organization and you are asked by a colleague for help, you must provide that help as quickly as humanly possible to everyone who asks.

One of the difficulties of working in semiflat (or falsely flat) organizations is that sometimes when people ask for help, they are left to twist in the wind. I have seen that occur far too frequently. I have watched as a bright, young associate in a large accounting and

---

Secrets of a Successful Flat Organization

- Encourage collegiality and respect among people within the organization.
- Make it clear that people have the authority to make decisions.
- If people have authority, then let them make decisions.
- Train them sufficiently so their decision-making skills are sound.
- Encourage a few common approaches to decision making.
- Allow people to feel sufficiently confident that they can ask others, at all levels in the organization, for help when making a tough call, and make certain they get that help quickly

---

consulting firm calls or messages a colleague to ask for help and receives no reply. I have watched as a young software developer struggles to fix a bug and calls a colleague who ridicules the request rather than helps. I have watched as a sales executive, with millions of dollars worth of orders on the line, calls a colleague to ask for help with a client who has a special request and does not receive an answer from that colleague. It is not that the colleague doesn't know the answer, but that the colleague is jealous of the size of the order.

The truth is, an organization is either flat or it's not. And if it is lucky enough to be flat, it will function well only if individuals can ask colleagues for advice, receive a quick and accurate reply, and be respected for asking for help.

BRINGING OUT THE BEST IN OTHERS

Even at the highest levels of an organization, the job of leaders is to bring out the best in the people on your team and to coach them into using all of their talents. But leadership is not coaching. Coaching focuses on helping people arrive at their own goals, whereas leadership, especially common purpose leadership, is about helping people arrive at a collective set of goals. It is about coordinating people's efforts, aims, ambitions, and capabilities.

This measure, though not inherently bad, sends the wrong message if only the CEO and a small handful of others are compensated this way. In my view, it is not just the CEO who creates value. The entire company creates value. I have seen, for example, people sleep overnight in their offices in order to design the best possible computer chip in the shortest amount of time. I have also seen people work around the clock to put together a great proposal or race through the day to make certain a plant's production targets are met. Do these people not create value? Is it only the CEO? Of course not. And yet how many times are these people compensated using the same metrics as the CEO? Hardly ever.

I am not arguing that everyone should be paid the same. Rather, I am arguing that pay and recognition must track with the common purpose concept that acknowledges everyone is a leader and everyone is a contributor. And yet there are certain areas where certain members of certain teams are responsible. If the CEO and CFO select the wrong capital structure and the company cannot invest as it should, this problem, which affects the whole company, was not the result of a screw-up in the paint shop. And, conversely, if a nozzle on a robot arm is not kept clean and replaced when worn, it is not the CEO or CFO who is responsible for parts that were painted incorrectly. In other words, everyone has a say and a share in creating value, and everyone runs the risk of destroying value as well. Because this is so, people must be rewarded for what they contribute to the enterprise as a whole. If only the CEO and his or her top team are paid that way, unhappiness will be widespread.

An old friend of mine, Bill Totten, an American who moved to Japan in the 1970s to start and run K. K. Ashisuto, one of Japan's top software distributors, explained to me that when his secretary arranged a meeting for him with a client, she was adding value to the company. "She's not just placing a phone call," he told me. "It's a relationship she's either starting for the company or maintaining or developing. That's extremely important, and it's something she should be rewarded for." Conversely, a number of us partners who worked at the New York headquarters of PricewaterhouseCoopers took it upon ourselves to explain to our security guards that when they were annoyed, short, or rude to people visiting the building, their actions destroyed measurable amounts of the firm's goodwill and value.

The simple but largely unrecognized fact is that everybody inside an organization is in the value-creation business. If the company stalls, if people are sitting in their offices or cubicles idly, don't blame them. Blame the organization's leaders.

The job of a leader is to set goals, measure progress, hold people accountable, and remove obstacles from each team member's path. This is not something that a leader can do on a part-time basis because he or she prefers wining and dining clients or solving complex logistics problems. Removing obstacles is a leader's full-time job.

I recall a meeting of CEOs at Microsoft talking to Anne Mulcahy, when she was chairman and CEO of Xerox. She explained to me as we ate lunch that the organization she inherited was fraught with problems. There were issues with regard to the accounting system, human resource issues (too many of this type of engineer, not enough of that type of engineer), product issues regarding quality, and falling sales. During her tenure, Mulcahy turned each of these issues around and transformed Xerox from the wounded giant of the document management business into a tough competitor. But as she described her business odyssey, she said something that was powerful: "The CEO's job is to help others in the company do their jobs."

This is a powerful insight. How can the CEO or any other high-level leader in a company the size of Xerox, which has about

$17 billion in revenue, do everyone's job? How can a CEO in a company that big even know what everyone is up to?

What Mulcahy had to do was set goals, measure progress, hold people accountable, and remove obstacles from their paths. To do that, she had to begin by listening to what people in her firm were saying. She had to hear what was pleasant and unpleasant, happy and sad.

Mulcahy and other CEOs are people of action. In fact, it's difficult for them to hear about a problem without lending a hand or putting together a group to create a solution. But the first step in solving a problem is making certain you understand the dimensions of the issue, which means listening actively so you are certain you really understand.

When I sat with Mulcahy, and later when we traveled with our group to Bill Gates's home by boat, I was impressed with how powerful she was as a listener, how curious she was, and how many questions she asked. She did not put her ego out front. She was not defensive in the least. What she did was scoop up as much information as she could from every encounter.

Leaders at all levels must remove obstacles from the paths of the people on their teams. But they cannot do that unless they are listening carefully to what each person says. Once they truly grasp the issues, they can act. As a result, I am convinced that one major component of Mulcahy's successful, multibillion-dollar turnaround of Xerox was her ability to listen—really listen—to what the other person said.

ACCESSIBILITY

It is important to be accessible to people within the firm and to engage with them in the right way so they exercise their own authority and learn. In many organizations, going to the CEO for advice is unusual, intimidating, and sometimes even career threatening. In most organizations, CEOs are not there to give advice. They are there to listen to your presentation and to make a decision that will affect your future. In many companies, the role of the CEO is financial: to listen to your pitch and allocate resources based on what you say.

At Continental Airlines, Gordon Bethune preserved his accessibility by making certain he invited people from the company at all levels to his office once a week for pizza lunches.

Before he was elected mayor of New York, Michael Bloomberg preserved his accessibility at Bloomberg LLP, the big financial information company he started, by putting his desk in the middle of the company's newsroom. Since he was in the center of the room, he could talk to anyone he needed to meet with, and they could talk to him. Not only that, but when people came to the company's headquarters to be interviewed, it was not unusual for Bloomberg to thank them personally as they left the room.

At many companies, CEOs and other leaders manage by "walking around," as it is called. While this helps the CEO get a sense of what's going on, it does little to create a true two-way communication approach, such as Subramaniam, Bethune, and Bloomberg developed in their respective organizations. The point of accessibility is to make it two way, to remove barriers to communication, and to make people understand that their leaders are part of the team.

Toxic CEOs

One CEO of an organization I know well has narrowed his role from visionary founder to that of what I can only call "chief spreadsheet officer." This CEO, who is unquestionably a brilliant financial thinker, brings in his direct reports, examines their numbers in minute detail, and barks orders with respect to operational activities that are likely to bring down costs.

But that's not the problem. The problem is that this CEO is so confrontational, rude, and brilliant that several of his direct reports have told me that often they are so nervous the night before meeting with him, they cannot sleep. One of his direct reports confided that she gets so nervous prior to her meetings that she has thrown up. Several times I have seen people go in to speak with this CEO smiling and come out so angry and frustrated that once they are out of earshot, they have punched the wall or gone into the bathroom to yell. The worst thing you can do, one of his direct reports said to me, is to say, "I'm not sure," or "I'll get back to you with an answer," or (God forbid!) "What do you think?" Even his board of directors is intimidated by him. And most often when a direct report makes a decision, this CEO overrules it or simply barks out, "No!"

The CEO I am referring to is almost a household name. He is well recognized for his wealth, philanthropy, editorials in the *Wall Street Journal*, and musings on the economy. But the companies his holding company runs have barely grown over the past decade, and the turnover rate of his top executives is atrocious. When I asked one of this CEO's business unit heads to name his most significant accomplishment, he simply said, "I survived." The sad fact regarding people who worked for this CEO was that they were almost all talented and smart. They came into the organization knowing it would be tough and left feeling defeated. The CEO often played on those feelings to negotiate deals that were heavily weighted on commissions or equity awards, and then he wouldn't make the awards.

This CEO may be an extreme case, but far too many leaders are like him in degrees. They look to their direct reports for only one thing: to help increase shareholder value so their own pay packages grow even fatter. These CEOs are members of a team of one. And in some ways, they even see themselves as working in opposition to their direct reports. Rather than viewing their teams as teams of leaders, these CEOs view them with mistrust and suspicion. They think the people working for them are incompetent, and these CEOs fear their teams will make them look bad before their boards and with their shareholders. And yet what can a CEO who is operating a team of one really accomplish? Can he or she create value? Change direction? Restructure the balance sheet? The answer is no.

While it may seem trite, the fact is that the best results come from people who treat others with respect, recognize their contributions, and enlist their help. It means trusting those you work with. And although not everyone is a genius, to be sure, not every job needs a genius's touch. A great deal of business is simply doing, on time and correctly, what you said you were going to do.

LEARNING CULTURE

Fortunately, not every CEO is like the one I just described and not every company is plagued by fear. Jeffrey Pfeffer, a professor at Stanford and an expert on human resources, recounted to me a good example of what I mean. In an interview in 2007 for a project for Mercer Human Resources, Pfeffer explained to me that when he worked with Anne Rhodes, at the time head of human resources at Southwest Airlines, he asked her why that airline had never had a layoff. She told him that if you really believe that people are your most important asset, "why would you put them on the street?" That perspective permeated the company, from the CEO all the way down.

If you believe in the value of your people, then you also believe it's worthwhile to educate them and keep them in the loop. If people are your most important asset, why would you want them to remain in the dark? You would educate them and train them and make certain they understood issues pertaining to their industry and company. You would spend money on them because that money would be returned out of their greater ability to create value.

Of course, there is a problem that is common even in organizations that call themselves learning organizations. "Everybody wants a learning organization," said Pfeffer. "But nobody wants an organization where anybody has any time to learn! It's a real contradiction. The reason is that if you are sitting around thinking and learning, people think you're idle." And yet what do people really do when they do business?

When I worked with Booz, Allen & Hamilton (now called Booz & Co.), the consulting firm, we went to great lengths to build up the firm's knowledge and learning tools. The reason was that people hire firms like Booz to solve complex problems, and to solve those problems you need to know a lot. Sitting around and studying, sharing what you learn, discussing, talking and arguing about solutions is how it's done—and there are no shortcuts.

At Booz, Chuck Lucier, the firm's first chief knowledge officer, was the first person to seriously track CEO tenure. He was the first to notice that CEO tenure was getting shorter from the late 1990s onward. Lucier developed a strategy for learning, discussing, and—sometimes—shouting about ideas. The first step comes when an individual, or a couple of individuals, got interested in a topic they thought might help a client. They might start talking about the idea after work and even do a little research into it. Then if it seemed that it was a worthwhile and practical idea, they would go to Lucier and ask for a little research money to look into the idea formally. If Lucier and his team thought the idea had merit, they would open up a research budget, knowing that most new ideas fizzle out.

If the research effort yielded some fruit, Lucier would make money available to hold a meeting, often face-to-face, in an office where five to ten people might discuss the topic in depth for as long as a day. And if the idea still had merit, they would create a formal interest group around the topic, holding a minimum of four meetings a year.

Lucier's approach proved to be very exciting. I recall a session in New York organized around a topic that focused on new ways of linking strategy to performance. The session began very abstractly. But Lucier kept pushing the fifteen or so participants to think about the idea from the point of view of the client. He also pushed them hard to be practical.

One senior consultant, an extremely erudite man with a Ph.D. in business and many years of experience working with manufacturing companies, stood up and began to talk about the idea. As he did, he used examples from various automobile companies, from parts manufacturers, and from an aerospace firm that were his clients. He talked about how great ideas have to tie lots of processes together the way all the tiny bones of a fish connect to its spine. In fact, he began talking about what he called his fishbone diagram to link strategy with all the different functions inside a company. As he spoke, you could feel the excitement in the air as a room full of very bright consultants went from 100,000 feet above reality, to 30,000 feet above it, to ground level. He made it all practical.

Soon after this meeting, Lucier organized some smaller meetings, and finally the product was proposed to two of the firm's banking clients—one in Canada and one in Germany. The two firms bought the idea, and the new idea began producing revenue. Even more important, it began to produce results for the client as market share improved and costs declined.

This approach was not easy. Start to finish, it took about six months to go from an interesting idea that was raised by two partners over a glass of beer to a multimillion-dollar assignment at two banks. And yet it shows what can happen when learning is applied and when all those clichés that say "we are a learning organization" become reality.

But there's more to the story. Lucier, as chief knowledge officer, functioned as a great leader, pushing session participants just hard enough to keep everyone focused and sharp. He used all his tools—his wit, intelligence, and ability to debate and argue—and he used his power over the budget to make things happen.

But leading a knowledge or learning organization is no different from leading any other type of organization. You need credentials. And Lucier had them, from the Ph.D. to a string of successes with clients. He was able to push, cajole, and argue, because he had earned the respect of his colleagues within the firm.

Companies cannot simply say they have a learning culture. They must have the wherewithal to make it happen. GE, perhaps the most famous learning culture company, has a management and training center called the John F. Welch Leadership Development Center at Crotonville, New York. The center, which opened its doors in 1956, is the corporate equivalent of the Harvard Business School. It teaches employees and customers the GE way of thinking and of analyzing and addressing problems. It offers courses in business management, leadership, finance, sales and marketing, and Six Sigma quality programs Work-Outs and Change Acceleration, to streamline operations and set strategy. When Jack Welch was GE's chairman and CEO, he often taught classes at the center, just as Jeff Immelt, GE's current chairman and CEO, does. (Today, among his many roles in "retirement," Welch is a special partner at Clayton, Dublier & Rice, where he applies many of the techniques he developed at GE to private companies owned by CD&R.) For a company like GE, with upward of $180 billion in revenue, its Crotonville Center is a requirement if it wants to remain competitive globally.

FM Global is many times smaller than GE. And yet it too recognizes that even smaller firms must continue to invest in learning if they are to grow. There is no other way for a flat organization with distributed decision to succeed over the long haul except by investing in its people.

Why a Learning Organization?

- Flat organizations require highly capable, highly skilled people to make decisions.
- Knowledge becomes obsolete faster than ever before.
- Leaders at all levels need to manage their careers themselves if they are to grow.
- The right types of education and training keep the goals of the individual and the organization aligned.
- Education and training ensure that an organization has the skills it needs for the future.
- If you extend training to include customers, as GE and FM Global do, you have longer relationships while teaching your clients to save you money.

It is no secret that some organizations scrimp on training. People come into those organizations with knowledge they developed at school or in other companies and essentially donate their knowledge to the organization. But after a while, the knowledge that people bring with them to the organization they join becomes obsolete. In fast-moving industries such as pharmaceuticals and software, the rate at which knowledge becomes obsolete is startlingly fast. In other companies, such as metals, mining, and industrial chemicals, the rate of change is much slower. Even so, no industry is immune from the need to update its knowledge.

At FM Global, the metaphor for an individual's career is the subway, complete with a map of courses and programs designed to look like a map of the London Underground. Not surprisingly, to keep the subway metaphor going, the system FM Global developed to help individuals manage their careers is called *Rail*. It's designed to make certain that each office around the world has people capable of fulfilling that office's objectives. So the Rail system not only helps individuals, but is directly connected to the firm's overall goals on a global, regional, and local level.

The big idea, according to Tom Lawson, one of FM Global's executive vice presidents, is to help people at FM Global manage their own careers and keep track of all the courses and training they've undertaken. But another big idea is to help leaders coach people within their groups so that each individual, team, and office is constantly upgrading its talent and capability in a balanced way.

At FM Global, learning is firmly anchored in its primary business mission: preventing losses. And like GE, it offers courses for employees and customers alike. For employees, there are in-structor-led courses in engineering and underwriting and many other offerings, including highly advanced engineering and risk management courses for professional. These course are offered online, in instructor-led classrooms, and as hybrids that have online and instructor-led components. In addition, Web-based courses are offered in real time with live instructors.

For clients, the list of courses, downloads, instructional videos, seminars, and classes is vast. The printed catalogue of course offer-ings, publications, downloads, and instructional material is forty-two pages, and the Web version is even longer.

Producing these publications, courses, and downloads is a sizable investment for all companies. But the returns are enormous if the training course tracks with the organization's aims. For clients at FM Global, that means helping prevent losses that FM Global must pay for. For employees, it means enabling people to manage their career for their own satisfaction and growth and provide the firm with the capabilities it needs to grow.

Leadership development is a critical component in FM Global's overall business strategy. And it's vital to creating a common purpose organization. Having a common language, or at least a common method of analysis and discussion, is an important element in building a common purpose organization. But to do that, you also need to have a lot of learning taking place involving as many people as possible. For the engineers at FM Global, the firm's sixteen-hundred-acre research campus and four main research labs give them access to the latest thinking in their discipline. Keeping engineers fresh and updated with respect to the latest innovations in their field is vital to retaining them. Enabling non-engineers to take engineering courses deepens their knowledge and helps them buy in to FM Global's approach to solving problems.

Common purpose does not just happen. It has to be developed and nurtured if it is going to thrive. But it cannot thrive if the organization attempting to embrace it is doing poorly. That means that whatever tools an organization selects to bring people together must be tied to the organization's overall business goals.

Chapter Seven

CREATING A CULTURE OF LEADERSHIP

GOAL SETTING

You cannot have a common purpose organization unless everyone is onboard with the same goals. That's not always easy. Building a firm of leaders can create vast reservoirs of strength, or it can end up as a team of rivals, as Doris Kearns Goodwin famously wrote in her book of that title about Abraham Lincoln. And while Lincoln is generally considered to be one of the greatest leaders in U.S. history, it did not come easy to him. In his administration during the Civil War, he was often far out ahead of his team. He was not a military man, and for the first years of the war, he was plagued by putting the wrong generals in charge. And yet he doggedly pursued his goal, changing generals and communicating better about the reasons for the war, until he found a leader who had the wherewithal to win the war.

I bring up Lincoln's struggles only because I believe we often assume that leadership is easier than it is. I also think (and this is not something that can be documented) that the issue of chemistry is important. Groups end up with the leaders they deserve, Warren Bennis once told me, and they reject those with whom there is no compatibility. Gil Amelio, a former CEO of Apple, Carly Fiorina, a former CEO of Hewlett Packard, and Mike Armstrong, a former CEO of AT&T, were all highly talented, high-energy, highly competent leaders—but not for the companies they led. All of them had short—or shortish, in the case of Fiorina—tenures. And all of them were rejected by the cultures of the organizations they were chosen to head.

Fit is an incredibly important and difficult-to-define attribute to select for when bringing people into an organization. In interviews, everyone is in sales mode. A check of references often turns up little. Character, honesty, and integrity are all very important aspects of a leader's personality, but two people who look the same and test the same way on paper are never interchangeable.

At the old Bell Labs, now Lucent, a study was undertaken to determine why some researchers become stars—even winning Nobel Prizes, in some cases—while others simply failed. People who were hired at the lab all had the same backgrounds. They were at the top of their classes at some of the world's best educational institutions, like MIT and Stanford. They had astronomically high IQs and had earned Ph.D.s. All of them were skilled at conducting research. On paper, they were pretty much equal. And yet some members of this gifted class of employees did not succeed. Some outright failed, some barely survived, and a few—may be 5 percent—became stars.

Two researchers, Robert Kelly and Janet Caplan, studied this phenomenon, and in 1993, I published their article on the topic, "How Bell Labs Creates Star Performers," in the *Harvard Business Review*. My takeaway from their research, which hardly does justice to their very thoughtful work, was pretty straightforward: star performers are people who know how to work with other people and can build networks of support within the organization.

This straightforward conclusion may have been difficult to arrive at, but it is not rocket science. No one operates in a company alone. We are all highly interdependent. In a company of leaders,

---

It Takes a Village in Business, Too

- Success is not a matter of IQ points; it's a matter of creating connections.
- At Bell Labs, stars were better than nonstars because they were able to build support networks within the organization.
- The ability to communicate with peers is a critical component of any individual's success.
- Organizations must train people to be better communicators.

---

preventing it from devolving into a company of rivals depends on helping people connect to one another.

When people pretty much know who everyone is, what everyone does, and where to go for help, then they know how to enlist others to help them succeed. These networks—sometimes gossip conduits, sometimes powerful ways of passing along best practices—must be cultivated. Common language, education, and learning culture help. But simply seeing people day in and day out is a factor too.

When I was at Booz & Co., I worked on a project that was designed to help banks achieve higher levels of productivity and profits. It was based on a complicated analysis of each region in which a bank operated. It started at the regional level, worked down to the division level, and finally ended with an analysis of each branch. We analyzed each area in which the bank operated and developed a scorecard that listed how all of the bank's organizational units were doing, so they could compare themselves to each other. As a result of that work, a manager in Sarasota could see how her bank did compared to a manager in Atlanta or Cincinnati. The aim of this project was to figure out what a bank's potential was in every area and then build a computer network that would allow best practices to be sent around the company so managers could learn from each other.

When we completed the analysis and presented our findings, we were very surprised by what happened. Before we could build the knowledge-sharing application, we discovered that branch managers around the country were calling each other to find out what they were doing to increase business. Without any prompting or new technology, the rankings alone were sufficient to prod each manager to use his or her informal network to learn how to take one region's winning approach and transfer it to their own.

Although we were all disappointed that we did not get to build the cool knowledge-sharing system that we had designed, we were struck by how leaders use their informal networks to share best practices and to learn what works and what doesn't. And, of course, those managers who were new, shy, lazy, or simply incapable of building a network were those who fared most poorly. And yet when people come in for an interview at a company, how often are they asked about their capacity to network? And how often do they ask in that interview how the company will help them build their network?

The answer is rarely.

Sometimes, Bennis explained, and I observed, you need certain basic requirements to build your leadership network. At Price-waterhouseCoopers (PwC), I admit that when I was hired to be the global lead partner for thought leadership and innovation, it came with a long and frustrating ramp-up.

First, I was not an accountant, and having the right pedigree was vital to becoming socialized within that vast organization once we sold the consulting firm. When I sat down to dinner with partners and heard them reminisce about how they came up through the ranks doing audits of Fortune 500 companies, I had very little to add. Having the experience of being an auditor created camaraderie among my partners and a wide range of common experiences and challenges. "We grew up together," I heard people say many times.

Second, while innovation creates revenue for a company's future, when I walked into PwC, I was confronted with the fact that most partners viewed revenue in the future as worth very little as compared to revenue today. No matter what I did, such as work on new and better ways to produce financial reports for companies and their investors, the challenge was to make people understand that ultimately these efforts would yield positive financial results for the firm. And while many companies tout innovation as their "most important product," the reality is that financially driven organizations have very little patience. Apple Computer may disprove this daily, with the release of one innovative product after another, but Apple is the exception.

Finally, in a vast, flat, decentralized organization like PwC, each large and small organizational unit, from the tax practice in Yorkshire, England, to the transaction services group in Shanghai, thinks it has all the answers. They believe, and often they are proved right, that innovation comes from being close to the client. How can someone based in New York or London create what the Shanghai team needs? There was very little belief that this could occur.

My challenge was right out of Kelly and Caplan's work: to create a powerful network that would allow me to interact with the organization's many parts, and to do that as a non-accountant and an outsider. I worked hard to accomplish this goal, and what I learned first was important. As long as I had the support of the firm's CEO, I had no trouble overcoming these obstacles. Aligning with the vision, goals, and mission of the top people in the organization helps leaders at every level. But when our CEO quit to become CEO of another company, my network fell apart, and I had to rebuild it painstakingly and almost from scratch. To do that, I had to munch my way through the firm—a breakfast with a partner in Boston, a dinner in New York, a lunch with a partner in London—which took time and, if the truth be told, added pounds of weight!

But over time, I accomplished my goals and was able to create a network that helped me get things done. Had I been at PwC for a tenure typical at FM Global, say, twenty-five years, my tasks would have been far easier. But one thing is certain: just as in the rest of life, you cannot succeed in an organization without a little help from your friends.

SOCIALIZING THE MESSAGE

Leaders can do a lot to get their messages out and build support for their plans. One of the best ways to do that is by bringing people together.

When he was CEO of Rhône-Poulenc from 1986 through 2001, Jean-René Fourtou would get together with his top sixty or so executives three times year. He wanted a frequency that would keep people in touch with each other but wouldn't be too intrusive. Meeting too many times takes away an executive's autonomy, he said. Usually these meetings took place in France, where Fourtou is from, and would have periods when the sessions were very informal.

Fourtou is from the Bordeaux region of France, one of its most important wine-producing areas. And because he is knowledgeable about the wines and food of the region, he would take time to do wine tastings with his managers and also share meals with them.

These sessions (if *session* is the right word) were opportunities to bond, elicit feedback, and share insights. They were opportunities to test ideas in a low-stakes environment. But they were also opportunities for Fourtou and his executives to get to know one another better.

I realize that to Americans, especially, the idea of wine tasting, sharing meals, and getting to know each other might seem counterproductive and perhaps even frivolous, especially in tough economic times. Americans like to be productive, or at least be busy.

But Fourtou's ways should not be dismissed out of hand. Getting to know the people you work with is important. After all, leaders depend on leaders to get things done, and you need to know each other's strengths, weaknesses, and interests. Getting insights into each of these could be done by questionnaire or by e-mail, I suppose, but to really understand others requires developing a relationship, which takes time.

Fourtou would give these relationships time to build. Then, as he explained, when a leader in Tokyo or Shanghai needs help, he or she knows who to call in Paris or New Jersey.

At Booz & Co., it was the same way. Each year, the firm held a partners' meeting that was part fun and part work. How well the firm did determined what type of an event was held. One year we met outside Washington, D.C., at a conference center, while another year (a much better year), the meetings took place on a cruise ship.

It is difficult to overstress how important it is for teams of people working together to meet informally from time to time. At Revolution Prep, the young, fast-growing company I mentioned previously, people working at the firm's Santa Monica headquarters office go out for beer together most Friday evenings. On special occasions—a senior team meeting—they gather at a karaoke bar.

The point is that you cannot lead if you do not know the people you are leading, and the best way to do that is informally.

At FM Global, in good times and in bad, senior executives at the beginning of the year travel to each of the firm's offices around the world to discuss the year's strategy, answer questions, and do something that is fun. So important are these meetings that FM Global decided to continue to hold them even in the economic downturn of 2009. In addition, they hold big conferences where

How FM Global Makes People Understand
They're Important

- Send the firm's top leaders around the world to meet with every employee face-to-face.
- Have the firm's leadership communicate the year's goals clearly, but also have them listen and take part in the ensuring discussion.
- Have the top people communicate the firm's culture everywhere.
- Hold conferences and meetings to celebrate and to train and educate people even in difficult economic times.
- Facilitate the process of leader-to-leader networking within the company.
- Make certain everyone has at least a little fun.

people can get together on a grand scale. "In one week, we hold two conferences back to back," Tom Lawson said. "We bring in 1,700 of our closest friends—850 for the first three days and 850 for the second. We do it even in bad economic times because it's an investment in our people and that's an investment we want make."

"They're cross-disciplinary, so we have client services teams mixed together with field engineers," Lawson said. "The theme is the evolution of excellence." There are presentations and discussions and opportunities to learn and interact. But there are questions too around the topic of "how have we evolved as a company," Lawson said. "How have we been able to make money in a year of hurricanes and tornados and economic downturns? And yet our combined ratio is tops. Discussing how we got where we are sets the stage for discussion of how we can get where we need to go against whatever conditions are out there." At these meetings, the leadership is deeply involved in discussing issues like excellence and execution and personal growth.

All of these events, and the expenses that go with them, are critical elements in how FM Global builds its common purpose culture. That culture is actually a set of relationships among leaders at every level. These relationships are complicated networks that transfer best practices. And as an organization, FM Global has gone to great lengths to help its employees create their networks, a conclusion that Kelly and Caplan say is a requirement for firms wishing to develop stars.

At FM Global, helping people develop these networks is not something that took place on its own. It developed because its leaders began with the understanding that FM Global is something special and that people within the firm are better off if they know each other and understand how they think and work. By creating opportunities for everyone to meet with Subramaniam, Bosman, Hall, and Lawson, the firm creates linkages around the world. And bringing people together at a big conference, even in an economic downturn, makes a very important point: the people working at FM Global are just as important as FM Global's profits, and maybe more important; the people working at FM Global are special, part of an important club with a set of common goals, ideas, and ideals. And, maybe most important, FM Global's leaders at all levels are people who can, and should, learn from each other.

"Leadership begins with a clear vision," Lawson said. "Then you have to communicate what you have to do to make that vision happen. But after you define that vision, you also have to examine where it breaks down and what you have to do about it when it does. And once you understand that, you have to create a business environment where people can be successful so they can execute against that vision.

"The business environment is important because you can have the best vision on the planet and still fail if the business environment is wrong. What do I mean by environment? To me, it means you promote an atmosphere where the direction is clear and where you can translate that vision into doable things—things you can give to your management team that they can actually go out, do, and accomplish.

"What I'm saying is you must translate vision into action. After you do that, you must make certain that the environment is both collegial and fun. But you must also make sure that your environment is one where people are accountable. That's what all our meetings around strategy and our big conferences do. That's what our educational and training system, Rail, does," Lawson said.

Chapter Eight

WE'RE ALL IN THIS TOGETHER

US VERSUS THEM

As I touched on in this book's opening chapter, often when referring to competitors, leaders resort to an us-versus-them strategy to rally the troops. And although it might work in baseball or football, it doesn't work outside the realm of sports. It's not that companies should not be competitive. They do need to maintain a vigil against all competitors and fight hard to win. But they cannot do it by focusing on a single adversary. That approach to leadership is doomed to fail. If leaders at Lowe's think only about Home Depot, or if Ford cannot get Toyota out of its mind, ultimately their enterprises will be doomed because they're focusing on the wrong thing. Rather than obsessing about the competition, organizations should focus on the people they want to serve.

I have seen too many examples of companies that focus on the competition only to lose sight of what they are.

Joe Rice III, a founder of Clayton, Dublier & Rice (CD&R), was one of the inventors of the leverage buyout industry. He's both thoughtful and modest. A Wesleyan graduate with a law degree from Harvard, Rice is no slouch. Over the years, he has raised and invested tens of billions of dollars and bought, fixed, and sold companies employing hundreds of thousands of people. His firm, like all other financial firms, has had its share of downs along with ups. But no one argues it is not a pioneer. And while Joe is extremely competitive—he was also a Marine—he spends very little time thinking about the competition. "We need to focus on what we do best and continue doing it," he said. "I'm interested in what other firms do, and I learn from them. But ultimately my focus has to be on us."

Rice, a man of principles and values, has turned down very attractive deals because "something didn't smell right," he said. For Rice, CD&R stands for something on its own, not in contradistinction to anyone else. He crafted the firm's values on what he and his partners believe (one of his partners is Jack Welch), not because it's fashionable or contrasts with what someone else is doing, but because it's right. This is the unusual world of high finance.

"We look at our values statement every few years," he said. "Most recently, we added respect for one another to our list of values. And then we put our money where our mouths were." He did so by dismissing a partner who was brilliant and successful but abusive to those around them. "It just wasn't the right way to be," Rice explained.

HIGH ROAD OF LEADERSHIP

Standing up for what you believe, versus standing up in an effort to prove you're not someone else, is the high road of leadership. It is also practical.

Over the many years that I have observed organizations, one constant rings true: when you've taken on an opponent and develop an us-versus-them culture, your opponent gets energized. Not only that, but your opponent then sees a justification and an opportunity to create a coalition against you.

I have a lot of admiration for Microsoft. But in its early years, it had an us-versus-them culture that saw every other company as either a rival predator or as prey. Microsoft competed hard, which is in no way bad, but it was unmerciful in setting itself up in opposition to everyone else in the war to control the desktop. Over the years, it used this strategy to win big battles that enabled it to dominate the spreadsheet and word processor markets. When it moved into the Internet, it took on Netscape and a no-holds-barred fight for supremacy. And it won.

But in winning, Microsoft also created huge opposition. Kleiner Perkins, one of the largest and most venerable venture capital firms, created an "anti Microsoft fund" that would provide funding for start-ups that attempted to eat around the edges of Microsoft's market. Other venture capital firms did the same. Google, a company much loved by people around the world for its "don't be evil" approach to business ethics, has decided to fight Microsoft by launching its own operating system, called Chrome.

In addition, some competitors, like Netscape, had powerful friends in Silicon Valley that were capable of organizing and agitating not just in California but in Washington, D.C. Soon, Microsoft's us-versus-them growth strategy ended with the Justice Department coming after it for unfair competitive practices. And while Microsoft may have decimated Netscape in the browser wars, once the government is against you, the fight is taken to a much higher level than just market share.

After hearings and expert testimony, the Justice Department during the Clinton administration decided Microsoft should be broken up. Not only was it not a good corporate citizen, it dominated too much of the market.

Some observers in the media and some analysts said the government's decision to break up Microsoft fell into the hands of chairman and CEO Bill Gates and Steve Ballmer, president of the company. They argued—unconvincingly, I might add—that if Microsoft became a Web company and a desktop company, it would create far more value than it would as a single firm.

Not only did I not buy that argument, but I was leading meetings at Microsoft headquarters when the news hit that the Justice Department had decided to dismember the giant software firm and separate it into at least two companies. Judging by the looks on Gates's and Ballmer's faces, this was not the outcome these two men wanted. The air was tense, the atmosphere was highly charged, and the mood filled with doom and gloom.

Through its early us-versus-them actions, Microsoft turned not just a company or two against itself; it turned an entire industry and even the government against it. Not only did it manage to do this in the United States, it did it globally. Governments in Europe especially wanted to get rid of Microsoft's dominance. The European Union sided against Microsoft and demanded that it open up its secret operating codes so others could write software to run on Windows. Governments in Germany, Spain, and France began migrating to open source platforms.

Circumstances dictated that Microsoft change. It negotiated with the government, became much more customer friendly, and stopped viewing the rest of the world as against it. Over time, the U.S. government backed down, and the Justice Department dropped its objections to the firm. But Europe's antipathy to Microsoft has remained in place.

Microsoft's us-versus-them approach had to be changed into a less belligerent approach before the company could go about its business without running into legal hurdles and resentment. Part of what Microsoft did was reach out to the communities in which it operates around the world. It developed programs for schools and health care centers, and it helped poor areas of the world with information technology needs. Although Microsoft embraced philanthropy, the company is quick to point out that it is doing it on a corporate basis and that the company's outreach efforts are in no way linked to those of its cofounder, Bill Gates, and the Bill and Melinda Gates Foundation.

Microsoft's links to the communities in which it operates are paying off by improving the image of the company. And while changing the image of the firm is worthwhile, one has to wonder at what cost. And, even more important, had the company approached its markets and its communities a little more gently, with a little less of the us-versus-them mentality, would it have had to change its image in the first place?

Microsoft is not the only example of what happens when leaders attempt to use an us-versus-them approach. Many companies that thought of themselves as underdogs or as the only firm that saw the light ended up with tire tracks on their collective backsides. After all, when you view the world as against you and treat every rival as a competitor to be crushed, you end up with all of your rivals having one thing in common: their hatred of you.

Us Versus Them and the Wrong Incentives

If you couple an us-versus-them strategy with the wrong incentive system, a leader can do a lot of damage to the organization. Incentives, as they are employed at many companies, such as Nucor, the innovative steel company, or Colgate-Palmolive, the consumer products company, give people a stake in the company's overall success. But at Lehman Brothers, the world was not only set up as us-versus-them, with "them" being the other great investment bank, Goldman Sachs, but the incentive system was skewed toward individual departments and away from the company as a whole. Not only was us-versus-them at Lehman a situation of Lehman versus other firms, it was also an us-versus-them situation of one department versus another, one person versus another.

Such a system where the incentives are set up to serve an individual's needs rather than the common good of the organization creates an environment where people will do anything to succeed. At Lehman, they were willing to borrow forty dollars from others for every dollar they put up on their own and were willing to take huge risks on derivatives and subprime mortgages. Lehman's methods not only produced a situation where there was no love for it in the financial community, they also made it heavy with risks. Finally, when it came time to bail out Lehman, Treasury Secretary Henry Paulson, a former Goldman Sachs CEO, figured the world would be better off without that venerable institution. His decision to let the company fail helped bring down the rest of the world's financial system. And if truth be told, many people speculate that the rivalry between Goldman and Lehman was partly responsible for Paulson's decision to let Lehman collapse. Certainly I have no knowledge about whether decades' worth of rivalry was in the back of Paulson's mind when he made his decision, but I can say that if you run your business so that you only make enemies, you better never need anyone else's help.

REAL COMPETITION

This is not to say that companies should be soft on the competition, only that they must stop short of hating their rivals and doing things to make their rivals hate them.

Great leaders are not those who press ever onward. They are people who are sensitive enough to know when to march and when to hold back. They understand what one of Israel's top military leaders once told me: "The best plans are those you can change." In other words, great leadership is not about keeping your competition in your sights and relentlessly pushing back your rivals. It is about keeping your customers or clients in your sights and doing everything you can, in a flexible way, to ensure you are committed to solving their problems.

In a common purpose organization like Joe Rice's CD&R, the truth is that highly competitive people hardly ever think about the competition. They are aware of their rivals, but they keep them in their peripheral vision. What great leaders think about are ways to make their own organization more responsive, flatter, better, and faster at achieving their goals.

NOT THE ART OF WAR

A great disservice was done to the field of leadership by pressing people to read *The Art of War* by Sun Tzu, which was trendy in the 1980s (and referenced with reverence in the movie *Wall Street*). While this is a great book with a powerful message and page after page of elegantly set out tactics, the problem is that most people look at this book and mistake a rival for the enemy. War is war— and very different from business. In war, your enemy is hidden on the other side of the hill and is waiting there to surprise and destroy you. Your enemy is an army or air force or navy, like you, and the match is like chess.

But in business, the enemy is more like the old comic strip character Pogo once said: "We have met the enemy and it is us." By that I mean that Toyota is not coming over the hill to destroy Volkswagen or Ford or Fiat. Toyota is coming over the hill to satisfy the needs of motorists around the world. Smashing Toyota with a head-on assault on that company is impossible. That's because war takes place head-on but business competition takes place at a ninety-degree angle. What I mean by that is that one company or firm succeeds against another not by attacking that company but by satisfying its own clients' needs. At PwC, we grew into the world's largest professional services firm not by antagonizing KPMG or

Deloitte & Touche and thereby uniting them, but by ignoring them and focusing on our clients. A head-on assault would have pitted us against our rivals in advertising, business pitches, and approach. Instead we emphasized our own qualities and strengths.

Great Leaders . . .

- Keep their competition in their peripheral vision.
- Focus on their customers, not their rivals.
- Set up programs so leaders at all levels can address the needs of their clients.
- Always strive to satisfy their customers' needs better than the competition does and than they did in the past.
- Study the competition—just not too much.

What we learned was that our clients were not interested in what we thought of our competitors. And they didn't care for pitches that explained why we were better than the firm they had used for twenty years. Nor did they care about the cool way (at least to us) we were organized, structured, or led. Rather, our clients, and our potential clients, were interested only in what we could do for them. If we were too aggressive against our rivals or maligned them, we would have made our clients very uncomfortable.

If instead we told a client how as a common purpose organization we can bring an army of highly skilled professionals together to solve any problem they have and that we can do it faster and cheaper and better than anyone else, they paid attention. Our clients wanted only one thing: great service. They didn't want to know what we thought about a rival.

So rather than fighting our rivals head-on, we took them on at a ninety-degree angle by focusing exclusively on satisfying the needs of our clients and organizing ourselves so we could serve those clients' needs. Everything we did was based on that, which is how we grew, how we decided to add services, and how we trained our people.

OTHER INDUSTRIES

It's difficult to think of any industry where focusing on bringing better service to your customer or client does not work. In the end, people want to have their needs satisfied at the right price. To that end, small things matter.

Sam Hill, a gifted and thoughtful consultant, analyst, and writer, once wrote an article that I published in *strategy + business* called "How to Brand Sand." The point of that piece was that even companies selling commodities can learn to outcompete their rivals in sectors where there was almost no product differentiation at all.

For leaders, Hill argued, the task was not simply to sell wheat or sand or salt or iron ore. It was not even to do it in ways that were cheaper than those of rivals. The challenge for leaders, Hill said, was to fulfill the needs of a client better than anyone else, even in a field as undifferentiated as selling wheat.

In his case study, Hill explained how Australian's Wheat Board was able to command premium prices not by undercutting American or Argentinean farmers, but by selling a product that had fewer impurities in it like tiny stones that baking companies had to sift through and remove on their own. By improving their product incrementally, Australian farmers sold their wheat at a higher price than the competition did.

Did the Australian Wheat Board have to understand its rivals' business models to take this approach? Of course they did. But did they have to focus on the competition and turn American and Argentinean growers into enemies? Not at all. Australian wheat producers became world leaders by focusing on their clients' needs and keeping their competitors in their peripheral vision.

The Challenge of Leadership

For leaders at all levels, this presents a challenge. Steve Wynn, creator of the successful and profitable Wynn Resorts, is interested only in creating an experience for his customers that his rivals cannot reproduce. Beyond that, he doesn't care very much what his rivals do. In practice, that means leadership at Wynn Resorts requires people who can make decisions at every level and can satisfy the needs of the customers. At the upper reaches of the organization, Wynn and his fellow leaders focus on the experience: Should guests be greeted by exploding volcanoes at the entrance or white tigers in the lobby? Should there be an art gallery or a wax museum? Should the rooms be highly decorated or spare? What do the customers want? How can they be thrilled in ways they never expected? What can you do to make them tell their friends about the great time they had when they go home?

I like to use examples from the luxury hospitality industry for a reason. What is it that they sell? If the truth be told, an upscale room is an upscale room and a casino is a casino. To turn what is in many ways a commodity into something that is a luxury takes more than taste when it comes to design and furnishings. It takes hiring, training, motivating, and leading people who can create great experiences for their guests but also connect with them.

In the hospitality business, one of the most important moments that occurs is when you first walk in the door. Does the bellman greet you? Does the desk attendant make you feel welcome? Does the hotel feel like a cold-as-ice eight-hundred-room behemoth with nice chandeliers and drapes, or does it feel like home? Or like staying with a friend? These experiences are the result of training. But they are also the result of connecting—or failing to connect. Leaders working in these surroundings have to staff their facilities and each individual job with people who connect on a human level. For this reason, hotels, casinos, and amusement parks are laboratories for creating experiences, for leadership, and for learning how to interact with people, and for doing it instantly.

But there is more. From a personal perspective, I have been a traveler for most of my life. I spent a good portion of my summers in hotels with my parents as a kid, and probably have averaged staying at least one or two nights a week in a hotel for the past thirty years. As a result, I have been able to observe this industry close up as a consumer, and I have come to understand its nuances. From that perspective, it has served as a wonderful laboratory from which to see how different people manage and lead.

Take Micky Arison, chairman of Carnival Lines and the Miami Heat. Arison said that in the ocean cruise business, which is similar to Wynn's resort business, he gives his leaders full autonomy to dazzle and entertain his customers. For a leader at Carnival, the job is to create brilliant experiences for people who go on vacation once a year. It is to make someone's vacations so memorable, and so much fun, that they think about and dream about it the entire year. Creating an experience that is memorable is how Carnival does well in good times and bad.

At the Ritz-Carlton, Simon Cooper argues for exactly the same objective. In Cooper's view, human capital, aligned with the organization's purpose, is an organization's most important asset. Creating common purpose even in an organization with locations around the world is vital to success. But doing that means enabling people to do their jobs.

Creating a great experience is not limited to the tour or hotel or casino businesses. It is something that leaders must do whether they are selling wheat or hotel rooms or airline seats. And increasingly it is something firms must do even if they are selling items like cars or computers. After all, Apple, one of the world's most admired companies, sells a product that differs from its rivals not in its capabilities but in the experience of tapping into those capabilities.

But not every aspect of the experience is equal. Some parts of it are more important than others. And it behooves leaders to understand which aspects the clients or customers appreciates and require most.

Contrarian Thinking

For many leaders, these ideas are contrary to their way of thinking. After all, many leaders rouse their troops by saying (or screaming), "Our competitors are in our rearview mirror and gaining on us. We've got to destroy them all and dominate the market!"

But energizing people by adding fear to their already substantial day-to-day pressures is a poor way to inspire them. Not only does it tend to make people desperate but, according to Richard Boyatzis, "Fear of failure may focus the mind, but it won't change behavior."

The reason fear and other negative emotions don't lead to positive change is that they close people down. "In the face of fear, people become defensive and resistant to change. In organizations where negative emotions predominate, people withhold information and rarely take chances. When fear predominates, creativity dwindles, individual initiative diminishes, and risk taking wanes. Corporate cultures can turn toxic," Boyatzis said.

Boyatzis contrasts them with positive emotions, which he views as far healthier for individuals and companies: "Positive emotions, like those associated with praise, have the effect of opening people up. When they are open, they are receptive to guidance, new ideas, and new ways of thought. When the atmosphere is positive, people are more likely to take risks."

This last point is quite important. Too many leaders think that if they create fear in the minds of their troops, if they make them very scared of the competition, they will create a culture of risk-taking warriors who will gladly do anything it takes to push the organization ahead.

Not so. From a leadership perspective, organizations have emotional lives. Some organizations are upbeat, and others are down.

I recall, for example, my first visit to Apple Computer. In the mid-1980s, not long after the launch of the first Mac, I was there to discuss how to make the company truly global, which meant introducing the Mac into developing countries around the world where power was intermittent, phone lines scarce, and money even scarcer. The idea I discussed with the company's senior leaders was to donate machines and network applications to developing countries so that the Mac architecture would form the information technology infrastructure in poor countries where most of the world's people live. Without going into the merits of my idea (it could have used a little more work!), suffice it to say that Apple embraced the idea and we arranged partnerships with some non-governmental organizations from around the world.

Back then, a number of things impressed me about Apple. First, they made decisions quickly. The fellow I was dealing with liked the idea and committed the company to the initiative on the spot. That told me that management was open, people had the power to decide, and leaders were everywhere throughout the firm. And when he made his decision, he didn't hem and haw. He embraced it. He was upbeat about it and decidedly positive.

Second, I was impressed by the energy of the place. People were excited about their work, about their jobs. They thought of themselves as revolutionaries, and they had posters and sayings in the offices and cubicles to that effect. They really believed computers would make the world better and that their computers would do it best. They were excited, not fearful, of the challenges ahead.

Third, I was impressed with all the bicycles I saw inside the offices. When people rode their bikes to work, they brought them inside the Apple offices and kept them in their cubicles. This told me that the culture was both youthful and informal. It also told me that people had interests—that they believed in fitness and exercise and they had a positive view of life. It was a joy to spend time in those offices.

Fourth, I was impressed by the creativity of the place. Everywhere I went, everyone I talked to was filled with great ideas. It was as if Steve Jobs's creativity and vision had permeated every molecule in the air and people were affected by it and emulated it. There was a lot of positive competition to think different, as one of its ad slogans said. And they embraced it.

And, finally, I was impressed with how much fun people were having. One fellow told me, for example, that he played volleyball every day at work. Apple's management had had sand brought in and dumped somewhere on the campus and turned the area into volleyball courts. He said they did it because that's the type of volleyball the people at Apple liked. Then he said to me he had done the same thing at his own house—replaced some of his lawn with sand—so he could have friends over from work to play beach volleyball.

In those days, Apple was a place for upbeat, creative leaders who were a touch fanatical about things—just like the company's cofounder, Steven Jobs. And what this showed me was the strength of Apple's culture and the power of an upbeat culture. (A few years later, when I met Jobs, I saw how much of Apple's culture was the result of his personality: smart, driven, upbeat, positive, creative, and a risk taker.)

To Boyatzis, one important objective of leadership is to create in people not only confidence in their ability to act on their own, but to help them achieve what he calls "cognitive agility." In other words, said Boyatzis, it's not enough to give people their jobs and let them own them. You have to create a positive culture so they can think for themselves. If, for example, one of Simon Cooper's desk agents at a Ritz-Carlton property is unable to figure out how to help an agitated guest calm down, the experience for the guest and the people surrounding that guest will be diminished. Creating the right climate so individuals can develop cognitive agility when faced with a problem is a vital and often ignored aspect of leadership.

Years of working within a fear-based organization, where all rival companies are viewed as foes that must be utterly and totally defeated, can shut people down and even limit their ability to solve problems. It's not that these people aren't smart. It's that they are so bogged down by fear and second-guessing—and whatever negative emotions are also tolerated inside their organizations—that they are too fearful to think, try new things, and be innovative and creative.

At CD&R, Rice's decision to respect the firm's list of core values is an important example of the way companies can shift from a negative to a positive emotional climate. By removing what might appear to be small things from what is considered acceptable, such as rude and abrupt behavior, being dismissive of new ideas, and lack of respect for colleagues, the atmosphere within an organization can become more positive. That seemingly small change can be very powerful. As Boyatzis explained, pointing out something negative gets people's attention, but people change only when they receive sufficient positive reinforcement to drop their defenses.

One company I continue to admire is Porsche. Porsche produces wonderful cars (I have owned several) and has been able to weather downturns, although it, like all other automobile companies, was hurt by the economic downturn of 2008–2009.

Under Porsche's former CEO, Wendelin Wiedeking, the company rebounded from a deep slump in the early 1990s and made bold, even audacious, moves, such as taking a majority stake in Volkswagen, a far larger company, and moving aggressively into new markets in the Middle East and China. Porsche's stake in VW proved to be a battle. The families that own major stakes in VW and Porsche are related, and the one trait they share is enmity. The two families hate each other. Even so, Porsche has made some big investment bets. And because its employees knew their CEO would protect them and protect their jobs even as the families feuded, they supported Wiedeking all the way.

Porsche employees knew that one of Wiedeking's jobs was to keep the atmosphere at the company positive, even as he continued forward with his objective (which ultimately failed) of controlling VW. And that's how it should be. A leader should make people understand that no matter how difficult the objective, they can achieve it.

Us Versus Them Within the Company

Consider Porsche's we're-all-in-it-together approach to labor relations versus that of what used to be called Detroit's Big Three: GM, Ford, and Chrysler. These once great companies were in more than one us-versus-them relationship. One of them was with their dealers. "I hate those GM guys," the president of one of GM's largest dealers and a former head of the dealer's association once told me off the record. "They force cars on us, they don't listen to what we hear from customers who walk into the showroom, and they build what they want to build, and after they stick us with those cars, they say to us, 'Now you go sell them.'"

It was also us-versus-them with suppliers. "Every time we go to the Big Three to sell them our products, they beat the crap out of us on price," said one major supplier I worked with on a Booz & Co. project. "Don't they understand that we're in this together? If they fail, we fail. If we produce bad products, it hurts them. If they can't sell cars, it hurts us. Shouldn't we cooperate more?"

And most egregious was the us-versus-them relationship that the automakers were involved in with their workers—the people closest to the product they sold. Every aspect of that relationship was adversarial. There were union leaders who hated the companies that employed their workers and automakers who hated the unions. For years, the negotiations were painful and long, with the union's aim being to squeeze from the companies the maximum no matter what doing so meant to the company's future.

So tense were these negotiations, so charged was the relationship, that I recall watching a PBS documentary on the auto industry, which was made in the 1970s, where one worker who ran a machine that lifted up car bodies for assembly explained that he "dropped" a car body onto the shop floor every once in a while to express his anger with the company that wrote him a check.

It's very difficult to create a smoothly functioning company where feelings of dissent, argument, disagreement, and outright hatred are the norm. Not only that, but acrimonious labor relations were not lost on the customer. When they saw strikes and disagreements, they became wary of buying cars made in such an environment.

Never-ending rancor, a feature of the old Big Three, was not something shared by companies operating outside the United States. It was a unique feature of the way the American car companies were built. In Japanese companies, whether in Japan or in plants transplanted to the United States, people worked together. At the Nissan plant in Smyrna, Tennessee, workers and managers wear the same uniforms, park next to each other in the same plant, and eat in the same cafeterias. Labor relations are smooth. At Toyota's plants in Kentucky, the same holds true.

Is it any wonder that the American car companies have had so much trouble selling cars and staying afloat? High levels of dissonance that come from the us-versus-them mentality bring with them huge costs. In fact, organizations caught in these types of negative behaviors rarely are able to recover. And if they can recover, it comes only when the rancor has ended. People do not, cannot, and will not operate at their best when they are in the midst of such turmoil.

And it's not just automobile makers. In many cities, like Los Angeles, teachers, their unions, and the school system have decided to wage war on one another. Rather than realizing they share a common fate, where the health of one is dependent on the other, the us-versus-them mentality has blinded them to that fact so they see only their own side. As a result, constant bickering, dissent, and anger have torn apart what was once the nation's top big-city school system and plunged it to the bottom of the list. Because of the toxic environment, many of the best teachers have left the profession. As a result, students suffer. New York, the nation's largest school system, graduated only 38.9 percent of its students from high school between 2002 and 2003. Los Angeles, the second largest school system, graduated only 44.2 percent of its students, and Chicago, the nation's third largest school system, graduated just 52.2 percent of its students, according to Christopher Swanson, director of research at Alliance for Excellence in Education, a think tank in Washington.

Rancorous organizations tend to perform poorly. Those that are harmonious, where people have fun and enjoy the work they do, perform better.

NEED FOR DISCIPLINE

Fixing organizations that have descended into the pit of us-versus-them thinking is not easy. In most cases, it requires getting rid of the people who have created the toxic environment in the first place. People whose default setting is anger or confrontation or excessive negativity need more than a training program, a few directives, and a pat on the back. Rarely have I seen such people transformed into common purpose leaders. For the good of the organization, these people should go and be allowed to find a place where their unique set of skills, not to mention their temperament, is needed, although I doubt such places exist.

Some time ago, I spoke with Jeffrey Pfeffer, a professor at Stanford who has studied leadership, management, and human resources for many years. He told me that after researching the Men's Warehouse, a large national chain of men's shops that have performed well and continued to expand in all types of market environments, he was struck by how that firm sometimes fired its best salespeople. The reason, Pfeffer explained, was that a star salesman could disrupt the team effort the company has tried so hard to create. Stars, for the most part, are out for themselves rather than the good of the firm. As a result, they can breed larger discord, disruption, and even jealousy. A star salesman can make a very good performer dissatisfied, so he or she loses her edge. Because of the negativity they can sow, star salesmen, while doing well for themselves, can bring down the overall sales figures for a store.

By creating an environment where *me* is more important than *we*, where it's us-versus-them, everyone suffers.

Chapter Nine

HOW LEADERS STAY POSITIVE AND DETERMINED

A LITTLE REALISM, PLEASE

So what should leaders do in the face of gloom? Should they sugarcoat the facts? Not at all. Individuals inside organizations can cope and succeed in tough times if they understand the reality of their situation and if they know, the way the workers at Porsche knew, they would be protected.

During the great economic downturn of 2008–2009, workers at one company after another lost heart and faith as many firms' top leaders continued to line their pockets while they were asked to sacrifice. Nothing is more disheartening than a tone-deaf leader who is offered a bonus and takes it, while the minions who produce products and offer services are penalized or dismissed. An excellent leader is one who is willing to go down with the ship. A great leader is one who is willing to give up everything to keep the ship from sinking. In a crisis, leaders at all levels must be given more authority, not less, to staff the bucket brigades to keep the ship afloat. But leaders at all levels must devote themselves with body and mind to saving the ship. During the worst part of the financial meltdown, Kenneth Chenault, chairman and CEO of American Express, told his troops to "define reality, give hope." To do that, he told me, he told them the company must "stay liquid, stay profitable, and invest" in projects that will gain market share. Few leaders have that level of determination.

THINKING TOGETHER, THE BOYATZIS WAY

I once worked with a major phone company that was trying to save $1 billion a year in costs. It turned out the company did not really understand its costs below the regional level. The financial guys working away at headquarters could say what the costs were on a state-by-state basis, but that was pretty much the smallest increment they could analyze. They looked at the world on a state-by-state basis because that was the way they were regulated and the way their rates were set by various public utility commissions around the country. But when this company began competing with others—cable TV companies that were offering phone service, Internet long-distance phone companies—they knew they had to do better. The company gave its managers a month to find the savings.

So if you have to cut $1 billion in expenses and you don't know very much about your costs, what do you do? My solution was to bring together the company's most seasoned regional operating managers and let them work through the problem. We met in a rural conference center away from the city in the middle of the phone company's massive territory. While the view of the mountains was beautiful, we did not leave our hermetically sealed conference room except for meals and to sleep. We were there to work.

I began by asking them to explain what they did, how they did it, and what they could do better, cheaper, and faster. These folks, experienced veterans, several of whom started their careers climbing telephone poles, had never gone through an exercise like this before. They were nervous and very protective of their budgets, and they weren't all that interested in sharing.

In facilitating these sessions, I made certain that the atmosphere was positive. I began by saying there were no wrong answers, no stupid questions, and no penalties for being wrong. I also said to them that the greatest savings might come from areas that they had not considered before, and I asked them to be creative, to take risks, to think differently. Then I told them a couple of lame jokes and showed a couple of slides of cartoons lifted from the *Harvard Business Review* showing people trying to solve problems. By this time, the mood was better but still far from bright.

When I explained our purpose and the goal of the meeting, I did see some of the thirty-five people in the room breathing a little easier and relaxing a bit more in their chairs. In fact, one regional manager with a thick southern accent confided to me at the coffee break that he thought the purpose of the meeting was either to "give each manager an RIF [reduction-in-force] list," which is to say, tell them how many of their people they would have to let go, "or simply to fire us."

To kick things off, I brought in three surprise guests: bankers. These bank regional managers knew nothing about phones beyond the fact that they used them. But they had gone through a similar exercise where they were asked to take out costs. I thought it might be helpful for the phone executives to hear how people in another industry thought about and attacked an equivalent set of problems. My aim was to lubricate their thinking and get them to look at the issues creatively.

At first, the "wire heads," which was how the telephone people referred to themselves, didn't see what the "money guys" had to offer. Their industries were very different. Telephones were heavy on infrastructure, engineering, and technology. They were a subscription service, and their prices were regulated, while bankers just pushed loans out the door, the wire heads said. In addition, the telephone guys argued, they had a near monopoly, whereas in banking, customers had many more options.

But as we discussed the banking case and as the bankers explained how their search for cost savings began with looking at the obvious and ended with an innovative solution, the wire heads became interested. Rather than simply cut costs, the bankers said, they decided on a riskier approach. They came up with a plan to bundle various products together—home loans, car loans, credit cards—which cut marketing costs but nevertheless added to revenue. The bankers explained that no one would have thought of bundling as an option when they first walked into a meeting group session.

"We were thinking, 'close branches, replace tellers with ATMs, reduce real estate, cut advertising,'" a money guy said. "Instead, we created a new way to sell, and by doing it, we reduced our costs." Then he added, "Our results have been phenomenal."

When the bankers left, there was grumbling once again among the regional managers about how different their industries were. Some members of the group looked downright depressed. But then a woman who had worked at the phone company her entire life and ran the largest and most rural region in the company's geography explained how she thought there was value in hearing from another industry that was saddled with similar problems to solve.

I was enormously relieved to hear her say that.

The group now began its deliberations by asking about things that seemed familiar to them. "What if we stopped buying our tools from Graybar [a wholesaler to the industry] and let our technicians buy them at the local Home Depot?" someone asked.

I had brought a group of four young nerds with me who sat in the back of the room hunched over their laptops. The nerds, three men and one woman, were fresh from business school, and their job was to try to calculate savings based on what they heard. My four nerds were armed with spreadsheet models and databases of assumptions. They had details on personnel, benefits, and aggregated expenses. They had head count numbers and rules and regulations governing revenue and expenses on a state-by-state basis. The nerds now ran the numbers on the swap-Graybar-for-Home-Depot proposal. "If we're generous in our assumptions," they concluded, "you'll probably save $1.2 million a year."

I wrote that figure on the whiteboard and cheerfully reminded the group that they still had to find $998.8 million in savings.

There was a lot of squirming and groaning and "woe are we" talk. After all, it took hours of discussion plus the insights of three bankers to arrive at what was basically a negligible number. "But at least we found something," someone in the room said.

I now asked the people to take us through some their processes. I asked them how they conducted business. Line maintenance received a lot of discussion, and then, in passing, someone mentioned the one maintenance call that really never went away no matter how much the system was upgraded: turning off the dial tone when a customer moved. For some reason, that caught the group's attention.

As we continued our discussion, a district leader explained the purpose and function of the dial tone and taught me that when a customer moved homes or offices, a technician had to drive to the location to switch off the dial tone. When someone else moved into the house, the technician drove back and turned on the dial tone. In rural areas where the population was not very dense and the distances were large, a technician might be able to take care of only one or two dial tones in a day.

Using rules of thumb, we then tried to calculate the average time it took to turn a dial tone off and on. It turned out—across the phone system, on average, and taking into account travel time—that it took nearly half a day of a technician's time to turn off an average dial tone and the same amount of time to turn it back on. And there were other costs resulting from the use of equipment and the cost of additional staff to take care of other matters while technicians turned dial tones on and off.

"Why do you do it?" I asked.

"To prevent dial tone theft," someone said. "If we didn't turn off the dial tone, someone could use the phone for free."

"And how much additional would it cost if someone made a call on a line that wasn't turned off?" I asked.

"Nothing," someone volunteered. "It's all up and running anyway."

Watching people in the room discuss this topic was like watching Jonas Salk discover the polio vaccine. They were animated and excited and could not wait to express an opinion. Their emotions were upbeat and spirited, and all traces of their initial gloominess disappeared. They had picked up the scent of what they knew would be big savings. As the group's mood became elevated, individuals started thinking creatively, and they took turns writing on the whiteboard, making their case.

Then a woman from the rural district stood up. Even before the nerds in the back could complete their calculations, she volunteered that her best guess from her back-of-the-envelope calculation was that each time a technician turned a dial tone off or on, it cost the company about eleven hundred dollars.

"How many times do you do that in a year?" I asked.

"About 4 percent of the population nationwide moves each year," someone volunteered. "We cover a region of about 22 million people with at least 600,000 unique businesses."

As the nerds in the back were doing the math, there was some debate about whether the cost of turning on and off the dial tone at a business cost the same as it did at a residence. There was further debate about how many lines were added or deleted a year for businesses and how many businesses moved. They decided that there was more turnover in businesses, about 10 percent, since they were so dynamic with new offices opening, some closing, new start-ups being launched, and some businesses failing. They did argue that businesses tended to be located in urban centers, where the time it took to send out a technician was less than in rural areas due to distances.

The nerds in the back calculated that if the company left the dial tone on when people or businesses moved, the phone company would save about $1.03 billion a year.

Not a bad result for the first day.

POSITIVITY HELPS COMMON PURPOSE

The point of recounting this story is not to show the brilliance of this group of leaders (or of the facilitator!). Rather, it is to show the power of common purpose and to remind readers of Boyatzis's view that negativity may focus the mind, but change—and, I would add, creativity—rarely happens unless the environment is positive and people are rewarded for taking chances.

Boyatzis calls the type of leadership required to make change happen *resonant leadership*. He calls it resonant because the leader, or leaders, are in tune with the organization and with each other. When he described the term to me, the image that went through my mind was of those tuning fork experiments you do when you are a kid. You take one tuning fork and strike it, and when you put it next to another tuning fork, the second tuning fork also begins to vibrate without having been struck.

In a common purpose organization, the power of a group that is in tune with each other is phenomenal. Not to sound too New Age, but when a small group of people within an organization are positive and in harmony and are accomplishing their goals, they set a tone that others follow.

A small group getting into harmony, like the one from the phone company, saved that company $1 billion a year and changed the way that firm conducted business and looked at its expenses. The power of small common purpose groups is immense, and others sense it. The work improves, the group gains cachet, and people who passed through those groups end up with a career boost.

To do Boyatzis justice, let me quote from an interview I had with him as part of a big research project I did for the human resource consulting firm Mercer called "Creating Value Through People": "A resonant leader establishes leadership relationships with the people around him where everybody feels in tune with each other. Resonant leaders tend to set a positive emotional tone overall, a sense of hope, that tends to be compassionate. They set up an environment where people care about each other and there tends to be a high degree of authenticity. Resonant leaders help the process of change move back and forth between what individuals need to be doing and what the team or organization needs. In sports, when you have a resonant leader, one of the things you notice is that the team improves as they get individuals improving."

This is quite a powerful insight and if I had not seen it operate myself, I would not have believed a leader in an organization could have such a powerful effect. And while these seem obvious to anyone who has taken the time to reflect, the important points Boyatzis makes are those that relate to the need for compassion, caring, and authenticity.

We are thinking, feeling, and doing creatures, so it is not enough for most of us to get a list of priorities and to then be told to go out and accomplish them. We need to be part of something, and we need to feel some measure of affiliation for the group of which we're part. In Boyatzis's view, compassion, caring, and authenticity have the power to bind us together so that we can do amazing things.

According to Joe Rice, a large part of his leadership success as a pioneer in the financial services industry comes from the fact that he has never put himself above the group he's part of, that he genuinely cares about the people who work with him, and he is authentic. And, as I previously mentioned, Rice is famous for turning down lucrative deals because they didn't fit with the company's goals, ethics, or what it stands for. And for Rice, those decisions were not agonizing. They were split-second, which went a long way to establishing Rice's authenticity and reputation for integrity within his firm and the industry he helped create.

Rice also is known for his caring. When I first met him, one of his young colleagues was diagnosed with cancer. The colleague was a gifted, bright young man with a young family, and his prognosis was poor. He was out of work a lot as he underwent chemotherapy. And yet where other cold-hearted financial firms might have sent him home, Rice kept his office ready for him to return and made it a point to connect with this colleague's family on a regular basis. And when his colleague's disease took a turn for the worse, Rice made certain that he knew his family would be protected.

I have heard stories about Rice helping people through all sorts of issues, including divorce. And all the while, everyone knew that his compassion and caring were real. Rice's firm is a tough competitor in the marketplace. But it is also a special place because of the resonance between the Rice and the leaders he works with.

When I asked Rice about his leadership style, he recounted his experience in the Marine Corps where *we* is far more important than *I*. "That bond never goes away," he said. "It's something that you always have. And I guess it's how I still operate. It's got to be about *we*, not *me*."

Rice not only built a firm; he built an industry.

FOUNDATIONS OF COMMON PURPOSE

My experience indicates that organizations without common purpose are far weaker than those with it. And why not? If powerful emotions like caring and compassion, along with values like authenticity, are the forces that hold these organizations together, what holds together non–common purpose organizations?

For the most part, they are held together not with the glue of caring and compassion, but with the paste of interesting work, various types of incentives, and money. Non–common purpose organizations need powerful retention packages where payments for an employee's accomplishments are stretched out into the future. But common purpose organizations need far less when it comes to these packages.

Let me make it clear that when it comes to common purpose and resonant leadership, one size does not fit all. People are individuals, and those who thrive in one firm might not thrive in another. Chemistry, fit, values, and many other qualities are in the eye of the beholder. And whereas some people might feel warm, fuzzy, and perfectly at home swimming in a shark tank, others need the warmth and calm of the beach. In my view, resonant leaders can create harmony only if the people they work with share a sufficient number of traits. That puts the selection process, whether for a team or an entire organization, into high relief.

DISSIDENCE

One of the reasons Boyatzis began his research was that he discovered that many organizations were saddled with very high levels of what he calls dissidence. By that, Boyatzis means that rather than getting things done, many organizations were beset by a culture in which disagreement, discord, and dissent were the norm. When asked to do something or when confronted with a problem to solve, too many organizations found themselves unable to act.

These organizations found themselves in a state of chronic disharmony. In this type of organizational climate, it was very difficult to get things done. Instead of action, there was argument. Instead of accomplishment, there was grumbling and groaning. Performance languished. The best people either left the organization or lost their sense of motivation.

What Boyatzis found was that a great deal of an organization's dissidence relates to the high levels of stress within the enterprise. "It is our contention," he said, "that the cumulative effect of chronic stress is that people become more dissident with themselves, their bodies, their families, their workplace. They lose touch, and then they eventually make bad decisions and become ineffective. They narrow their view."

Imagine an organization that, when confronted with a challenge, narrows its scope and diminishes its creativity. Imagine an organization that, when confronted with adversity, becomes worse, not better, at problem solving.

Boyatzis studied this phenomenon for nearly thirty years, and his conclusions were that "if you really look at the data it consistently says that 50 percent of people in management and leadership

---

The Stressed-Out Organization

- There are two types of stress: negative and positive.
- Positive stress is associated with the challenge of achieving a goal.
- Negative stress results from leaders' and managers' negating other members of their teams, micromanaging them, overlooking them, and giving them challenges that are too small.
- Negative stress occurs when people are not listened to.
- Negative stress creates organizations that are less resilient and less adaptable and that fail at problem solving.
- Negatively stressed organizations are toxic organizations.
- Negatively stressed organizations can be unhealthy organizations in which people actually fall physically ill because of the way they are led.

positions are detracting from an organization's value. Another 20 to 30 percent in management and leadership positions are neither adding nor subtracting value. You can take these people out of the organization, and it would probably function more effectively. The fact is that the people who are adding the most value are only the top 5 percent or so. In a really high-performing organization like GE of the 1980s, it might be as high as 10 percent. But the research indicates it's never more than that." Boyatzis's conclusion is nothing less than shocking, and it is amazing that it has not received more attention.

It is easy to understand intuitively how stressed-out organizations fail. The essential leadership glue of compassion, caring, and authenticity gets lost in the shuffle as stressed-out people scramble over each other and confront high levels of organizational push-back to get things done. People cope, but they don't end up leading very well, and the best people depart the organization over time. In organizations like these, the talent pool gets thinned, the ideas diminish, and the organization fails.

Let me be clear, however, that not all stress is equal. We have known since the 1930s, from the pioneering research of Hans Selye in Canada, that some stress is positive. Positive stress is the type of stress you sometimes feel when you are excited about achieving a goal or a project. An athlete training hard for a sporting event might feel this type of stress as he or she struggles each day to achieve higher levels of endurance, strength, accuracy, or speed. A student studying to master a topic in which he or she is interested can also feel positive stress. People working in organizations who are stretching to achieve new goals might feel positive stress.

Negative stress is different. It's the one we feel when we are fearful or angry or under pressure to perform in a manner we don't agree with. It is the type of stress we feel when someone we report to just doesn't "get us," or "see us," or respect us—when the person we report to doesn't listen to our views. It is the type of stress people feel when, paradoxically, they are not given enough to do or when they are ignored. This type of stress can make people feel depressed or demotivated or hopeless or bored.

According to Boyatzis, people need challenges in order to perform at their best. They need direction, but, just as important, they need to be left alone to accomplish their goals.

In our new employment compact era, where loyalty is based on performance, why not allow the people on your teams to succeed or fail on their own? Why not let them own their jobs? In a flat organization, micromanaging is not only counterproductive and just plain stupid, it is destructive to the individual's sense of well-being because it creates high levels of negative stress.

When a firm is awash in negative stress, "it actually has a sclerotic effect on the organization and the organization becomes less adaptive and less resilient," Boyatzis said. "The effect of this kind of stress within the organization is that there is actually a physiological response among individuals. Their sympathetic nervous system changes, which means they're literally getting poisoned by their organizational environment," he said.

The cause of these problems is poor leadership. A toxic, dissident leader "refocuses everyone on a narrower and narrower spectrum of performance. Most common is that this type of leader makes everyone focus almost entirely on the financials. Now, obviously, you have to manage the financials. But not to the exclusion of everything else," Boyatzis said.

What all this suggests is that making people feel small, forcing them to narrow their focus, restricting their creativity, and limiting their ability to contribute are among the most toxic forms of leadership anyone can devise. And although people need to focus, there is a difference between focusing and mindlessly forcing other members of your team to restrict their view. Forcing people into smaller and smaller boxes is not only damaging to the organization, according to Boyatzis; it can even make people sick.

While Boyatzis has data to back up his assertion, I must say I have seen his conclusion play out in real life. One financier I know bought dozens of companies in the 1990s. His perspective was exclusively financial, to the extent that when people tried to engage him in a conversation about strategy or quality or even brand, he would become angry at their loss of focus. "Our job is to make money," he would say, "not pretend we're consultants." As a result, he forced all of the people on his team, and all of the CEOs of the businesses he bought, to focus only and incessantly on the financials.

What was the result? Over a period of six years, the financier saw an exodus of talent at all levels from his companies and from his firm. He lost almost all of his CEOs, his best analysts, and several of his business partners. During that period, a number of the companies he bought went bust, and it took him almost four years to sort them out: selling some, closing down others, and finding new talent to lead the ones that remained.

During that period, as I attempted to work with the financier, I observed some things that were either curious coincidences, requiring further study, or that confirmed Boyatzis's view. People in the financier's highly stressful headquarters office and in his operating businesses complained that they were sick all the time. They did this so much that theories began to develop in the office with people saying they thought there might be mold in the building or a faulty ventilation system. Some people said that they thought it was a "sick building."

No one that I know of at the firm died unexpectedly or suffered from the onset of some grave illness. But no one was happy either or felt at ease. Everyone in that company and in the companies that were acquired felt ill at ease, stressed, and unhappy.

As I wandered the halls talking to people, it often struck me that we should not simply tolerate our jobs, the way we tolerate a bad-tasting medicine when we're sick. We should enjoy them. Our jobs take up a large portion of our lives. What this says is that we shouldn't just put up with them. We should find them exciting and challenging, and although there is no such thing as stress-free work, the majority of that stress should be positive.

In a recessionary period or even in a run-of-the-mill downturn, our choices are often limited. But when jobs are plentiful and the world is growing, it behooves us to lead in a positive way and to work with leaders who do the same. And while we might not all be geniuses, most of us are sufficiently capable that our talents can find a worthy home in more than one setting. If that is true, and I believe it is, then why accept working with people who create a toxic environment? Why not seek out people whose aim is to create a common purpose organization?

Chapter Ten

LEADING IS A MENTAL GAME

USING POWER

Even in flat organizations, it's a given that some people have more power than others. People have different spans of responsibility, and they must have the tools to perform that task for which they are held accountable. Leaders need those tools, and some of them come in the form of spans of control. CFOs need to exert authority over the way the financials are reported, marketing people need to create and protect the firm's brand and image, and board members need to protect the interests of the share-holders. But organizations are not kingdoms, and power within organizations must be limited.

In a common purpose organization, good decisions get better when people have a chance to deliberate. Since internal rivalries are rare and everyone shares in the success of the organization as a whole, it makes sense to think things through and ask peers for their help and advice.

In many organizations, however, asking for help is a sign of weakness. Leaders must be watchful for that belief and deal with it brutally. Organizations grow and become more competent when information is exchanged. Consider how powerful it is to the organization as a whole when any employee can walk into the chairman/CEO's office and ask for advice. Not only does it send a message throughout the firm; it transfers knowledge.

Using leadership to transfer knowledge is a huge and powerful secret that some organizations grasp and others do not. At Wynn Resorts, asking people to communicate with each other about how they helped guests not only celebrates individual efforts; it transfers knowledge informally. People see what their peers are doing and copy that behavior. What this means is that one big focus for leaders must be to make certain the organization enhances its ability to act.

Art Schneiderman, a former consultant who worked at Analog Devices, the big chip maker in Boston, devised a way to use scorecards to analyze learning within companies. Schneiderman's thesis was that gains in efficiency and effectiveness are really indicators of how quickly a firm learns. He created scorecards for performance metrics that charted quality, delivery times, customer satisfaction, and other factors like percentage of revenue derived from new products.

In Schneiderman's view, a company like Analog Devices, which faced competition from around the world, had to view its main job as becoming smarter than its rivals and faster at implementing what it learned than any other firm. By looking at performance metrics as indicators of learning, he was able to directly connect training with corporate performance. For the leaders at Analog Devices, which has been a leader in specialized chip design and fabrication for more than two decades, Schneiderman's metrics were a godsend. Suddenly, by using these scorecards, Analog's senior leaders could shift the firm's emphasis and output by enhancing what it knows and by creating tools, like workshops, to transfer knowledge. The firm's leadership position in the marketplace was intimately tied to its leadership and commitment to learning.

LEARNING AND LEADING

It may be a bit unusual to equate leadership and learning. And yet as Analog Devices illustrates, great leadership requires not only a respect for learning but access to learning tools. FM Global and Analog are big enough firms to devise their own programs. But other great organizations find ways to marry leadership and learning.

One of my favorite cities is Kyoto, Japan, a remarkable city with wonderful architecture, cherry trees galore, and fascinating Zen gardens. On one trip, my hosts, a group of Japanese automobile executives, took me to a Italian restaurant. I was perplexed. Here we were in the center of old Japan, with traditional restaurants, tea shops, and *ryokans* (traditional Japanese hotels), and my hosts wanted to eat Italian food? Did they think I was so unrefined and provincial that I had no appreciation of Japanese cuisine?

Actually the reason they wanted to take me to this restaurant was to show me something they thought was important about leadership. The restaurant, which looked like a traditional Japanese restaurant on the outside, was very Italian on the inside, with warm pastel colors, white tablecloths, candles, and Western flatware rather than chopsticks.

I remember having a pasta dish and a veal entrée. The sauces were delicate and very much like what I had eaten in northern Italy. The pairing of wines was impeccable. And the selection of Italian wines was vast. It was a wonderful dining experience. But why an Italian restaurant? I asked my hosts.

"We wanted to show you something special," one of my hosts said, a senior manager at one of Japan's biggest automakers. "We think it provides a good lesson about leadership."

"Which is?" I asked, leaning in and savoring the last drops of wine.

"Once a year, the owner of this restaurant closes his doors for ten days and takes all of his employees on a trip to Italy. They go to a different region each year. The waiters go, the chefs go, even the dishwashers go. As they travel the country, they of course pay attention to the food. But they also pay attention to the ambiance, to the way the plates are prepared, to the service, and to the way each different food is served. They go to Italy for the experience, and when they return, they recreate that experience in this restaurant."

"Isn't that quite expensive?" I asked.

"Yes," my host replied. "But when the owner and the restaurant staff return, everyone in town is excited about what they learned and about the new dishes they will soon be serving. Business always picks up," he noted.

In addition, these visits to Italy rebuild the restaurant's esprit de corps. Everyone who works there feels special—as if they are on a mission on behalf of their clients to discover what will delight them.

The restaurant's owner is not a wealthy man. Closing his doors for almost two weeks comes at a price. But he decided when he opened his restaurant that he wanted it to be the best and most authentic Italian restaurant in Kyoto—perhaps in all of Japan. He wanted his restaurant to be authentic not just with regard to cuisine, but also with regard to the experience he provided to his guests. As a leader, it was explained to me, the owner did not really care that his restaurant cost more to run than other restaurants that got their recipes from books. He knew that by making a regular pilgrimage to Italy, he was creating a mystique for his endeavor and that customers would pay more for the experience of tasting something novel and good.

But the real surprise was that an executive at a global, multi-billion-dollar Japanese automaker would care about a business as small as a restaurant with only one branch as an example of how people should lead.

"I take a lot of people to this restaurant," he told me. "I take dealers from around the world, suppliers, managers from different geographies. Sometimes I think I'm the one keeping this restaurant in business," he told me with a smile. "But it's an important lesson. It's not the size of an organization that matters. It's how it is led and run. And for that reason, I bring people here."

The lesson from the Italian restaurant in Kyoto was that real leadership is a resource that is largely based on knowledge, and that knowledge must renewed. What you learned in college or graduate school, what you learned on your first job, might form the basis for how you lead. But you must make "pilgrimages" on a regular basis to see what innovative leaders are doing.

At Analog Devices, one piece of knowledge that Schneiderman uncovered was that knowledge comes with a half-life. What worked yesterday works less well today and won't work at all tomorrow. As a result, training must evolve, learning must evolve, ways of doing and leading must evolve, and even the way the organization is structured must evolve. A clever scorecard can keep track of how the process of renewing knowledge is going. But at its heart, knowledge must be constantly renewed so that leaders have the tools they need to build and rebuild the organization so that its performance always improves.

WHO LEADS? WHO FOLLOWS?

Michael Maccoby, a brilliant student of leadership and psychology who is also a psychoanalyst, told me once that the definition of a leader should be simple. A leader, he said, is someone whom people follow. And while common purpose leaders are people whom others align with in the pursuit of common goals, Maccoby's definition makes sense. Leaders have followers, or, at least, leaders have people who join them in pursuit of a goal.

In Maccoby's view, some people follow leaders out of fear. If you lived in Iraq during Saddam Hussein's rule, Maccoby argued, you probably did what Saddam said out of fear. The list of leaders whom people follow out of fear is probably endless. Ruthlessness is, after all, a peculiarly human trait.

The fear factor can be big or small. Maccoby speculated in a lecture, for example, that during the 2004 U.S. presidential election, President Bush used the color-coded terrorist warning system to scare people into voting for him by personally changing the threat level colors from yellow to orange when he needed to boost his popularity. Although Maccoby's contention regarding Bush's use of the threat-level system has not been proven, it does offer a good example of the types of tools a fear-promoting leader might use to arouse followers.

There are other types of leaders, of course. Many people follow religious leaders out of love, devotion, or respect. This form of leadership, while flattering to the person at the center of attention, is dangerous. Jim Jones, a religious cult leader, took his flock of devoted followers from San Francisco to Guyana where he convinced them to drink Kool-Aid laced with cyanide. The result of Jones's leadership was the death of 909 people who were lured into killing themselves out of love and blind devotion.

To my mind, following leaders is dangerous at best. The world went on record in the aftermath of World War II, during the Nuremberg trials, that mindless followership can sometimes end in the commitment of heinous crimes. To that end, it was decided that followership is no excuse for wrongdoing, even when one is following the will of an elected leader. At Nuremberg, it was further decided that we are responsible for our actions, no matter the circumstance. If the path of followership leads to destruction, we are morally obliged to abandon any leader who guides us in that direction. We cannot justify bad behavior by saying we did it because we were told to. In the end, we are responsible for our actions, no matter which organization we join, no matter which leader is in charge.

It is important to say this because followership can be quite dangerous when following someone means surrendering our judgment, not to mention our will. In my view, any time we must surrender our will to a leader or the group, something is wrong. For that reason, I am far more comfortable when individuals align their interests in the pursuit of a goal and do so without surrendering their right to voice an opinion, oppose a decision, or, if need be, withdraw from the group. Organizations that are not afraid to brook dissent are among the most powerful and long-living organizations around. The motto "Think," which has guided IBM for more than half a century, is powerful and compelling because it is respectful of the individual and his or her ability to contribute. And while an organization that asks people to think may be messier and more clamorous than one that requires them to obey, IBM's long-running success is testament to the power that can be generated when free-thinking individuals align their interests in pursuit of a goal.

There are more benign and powerful forms of leadership than those that require followership. Among the most striking are those that focus on values and competencies. Gordon Bethune was a values-and-competency-based leader when he was chairman and CEO of Continental Airlines.

During Bethune's tenure at the airline, it was not uncommon for people to say they left their job with another air carrier because they wanted the experience of having worked with Bethune. By doing so, they said, they would develop their own leadership skills while deepening their industry knowledge. In some ways, Bethune comes closest to a leader people want to follow, or at least align with, in order to learn things. And in some ways, one of Bethune's most powerful strengths was that he looked at his teams as teams of equals. True, Bethune was at the helm and the ultimate decider if it came to that, but he was never an autocrat. In the high-tech, high-risk world of commercial aviation, even a CEO knows that when a pilot is flying a plane filled with four hundred passengers through the air at 600 miles per hour, the views of the CEO are not particularly relevant. Everyone working at the airline must do his or her part using all of their powers and judgment in service of a common goal. By setting goals and then allowing people to achieve them, Bethune's leadership style was powerful, and successful, because it was based on mutual respect.

While all types of leaders have their adherents, those like Bethune are among the most valuable. They advance the organization because they understand that mutual respect, learning, and building common purpose are the basis of everything they do. And because they are open and share that purpose with others (not to mention the sharing the rewards), they create an environment in which people are able to develop and are willing to sacrifice for the good of the organization.

Leaders like Bethune understand that they have no divine right to wield power (Bethune began his career as a mechanic in the army, not as a graduate of an elite school) and cannot wield it effectively in a highly politicized or toxic environment—but not because of some divine right. Rather, they understand that their power comes from enhancing the abilities and opportunities of others and from removing obstacles that may litter the organization's pathways.

In the end, Bethune's staying power at Continental was not based simply on how he treated others. It was based on the fact that the way he led resulted in a company that outperformed its competitors and created value for its passengers, shareholders, and employees. In my view, while leadership is about building common purpose, it is also about building high levels of performance. Ultimately one of the greatest highs a team can feel is when its performance exceeded everyone's expectations, including its own.

Leaders who help their teams achieve aims beyond their expectations find that they have no difficulty recruiting people to join them. And why not? In our free-agent, new-employment-compact world, where loyalty is no longer the virtue it once was, being a member of an organization's top-performing team means you will always be in demand. It is no surprise, for example, that the three runners-up to succeed Jack Welch at GE all became CEOs of large companies. Working on a great team, with great leaders, provides a boost to any individual's career.

WHY PEOPLE FOLLOW NOW

Even more important than working with a leader from whom you can learn, argues Maccoby, is working with a leader whose purpose you share. In our highly interactive world, people are far less interested in following someone than they were in the past. In our knowledge-driven society, Maccoby argues, people want to collaborate.

Years ago, when people stayed at a company for most of their careers, they came up through the ranks by doing what their superiors said. In those days, before everyone was linked together electronically and on the Web, knowledge was far from democratized. Rather than sharing information, people at the top of an organization developed it, hoarded it, and doled it out bit by bit. Back then, said Chuck Lucier, a senior strategy partner at Booz & Co., sharing knowledge was considered unnatural. The structure of organizations, at least until the early 1990s, meant that there were leaders and there were followers, and almost by definition, followers had far less information than their leaders. Because followers took it as a given that their leaders knew more than they did, they would sometimes find themselves obeying a command with which they disagreed and justifying it by telling themselves that their leaders knew more.

Today, with information so widely dispersed and available, that model exists only in anachronistic, control-oriented organizations. In most organizations today, people are awash in knowledge. And since the information-playing field is far more level than ever before, collaboration is a far more appropriate working relationship than followership.

But I go Maccoby one further. Rather than collaboration, I like the concept of alignment to define the working relationship. I like it because alignment implies that work takes place between individuals who are equal and are acting on their own initiative in pursuit of a common goal. This, after all, is why organizations are formed: to achieve goals that are beyond the scope of an individual working alone. The concept of alignment simply calls attention to this fact.

While this may seem like a subtle or even a semantic difference, it seems to me that the word *alignment* is well suited to describe a period in which the new employment compact prevails. I say that because people in organizations are neither owned nor indentured. They are free to join and free to leave. And whereas collaboration sounds transactional or even project related, alignment is a deeper concept that suggests individuals voluntarily putting themselves on the line for tasks of longer duration.

TYPES OF LEADERS

Maccoby suggests that there are three distinct types of leadership roles within organizations, a view with which I agree:

- Strategic leaders
- Operational leaders
- Bridge-building leaders

Strategic leaders are people within organizations who plot the course. They are the longer-term thinkers. This type of team leader, in the guise of a CEO or business unit head, for instance, works with a group to set a firm's overall goal. He or she does this the way the captain of a ship plots a course, working with the navigator and other members of the crew to determine where the ship should go, what course it should take, and how much fuel it needs to get there.

Strategic leaders generally can think far into the future. Most often they possess analytical skills, and many are highly skilled with numbers. If they work with technology, they are people who understand not just today's technology, but how it is evolving and what might replace it along the way. These are people like Marc Benioff, founder of Salesforce.com who, in the age of the desktop when working for Oracle, foresaw networking and who, in the age of the network, foresaw Web-based applications, and in the age of Web-based applications, foresaw cloud computing.

The best of these people understand where the future is going and how to get there. Many of these people (the ones I really admire) view change with a sense of play. They love trying to figure out tomorrow's challenges long before they happen.

While CEOs and their teams usually take on the strategic leadership role, this type of leader is needed at many more levels than simply at the top. While Micky Arison, chairman of Carnival Cruises, might own his firm's top role as strategic leader, other people in the organization also have strategic responsibilities. Brand management, talent management, entertainment director: each of these positions also has a strategic role.

In the military, overall global strategy might be the purview of the secretary of defense. But in addition to the secretary, there are generals with responsibility for different theaters of operation and sergeants who, in the thick of battle, assume the strategic role. The point is that strategic leaders are needed at all levels.

One of the most brilliant strategic leaders I know, Michael Milken, never ran a company. In his heyday at Drexel, Burnham & Lambert in 1980, he provided credit to hundreds of companies and helped them pursue their plans. In the process, he helped companies assess their options, develop new capital structures, and focus on their markets. By doing so, he provided funds that companies used to create the cable TV industry, the cell phone industry, much of the modern homebuilding industry, and a great deal of the gaming industry. Creating industries requires a long-term perspective about where the world is going. Providing $200 billion in capital and detailed analytical advice about the future so other leaders can pursue their dreams requires deep knowledge and a sense of where the world is heading. And yet Milken never functioned as a CEO and never was chairman of his firm. He was a department head working from a satellite office in Beverly Hills for a firm head-quartered in New York. Strategic leadership needs to be everywhere and at all levels in the organization.

The role of operational leaders is quite different from those of strategic leaders. Operational leaders make certain the trains run on time, the manufacturing processes are adequate, the logistics systems work, the technicians are well trained, and the trucks are where they are supposed to be. Some organizations emphasize operations over strategic leadership. For others, the reverse is true. But like strategic leaders, operational leaders are vital to an organization's success.

In slow-changing industries, such as the telephone industry prior to the breakup of the old AT&T near-monopoly in 1984, strategy was far less important than operations. Prior to its breakup, Ma Bell had essentially no competition, its rates were set on a state-by-state basis, and no one was trying to drive it out of business by out-innovating the company.

Under those circumstances, what mattered was operational excellence. The system and its phone network was built, then overbuilt. For the operational wire heads who ran Ma Bell, the objective was to make certain the system would never go down, no matter how many people used it. As a result, to make certain the system worked, Ma Bell's operational experts designed the entire system so it would work flawlessly no matter how much voice traffic it had. For engineers, technicians, and systems designers, there was no better place to work than at the old AT&T. It was an operational leader's dream.

When the company was broken up, the landscaped changed. New competitors like MCI emerged with strategic rather than operational leaders at the helm, a shift in leadership that left Ma Bell reeling. MCI, the so-called Baby Bells (a group of regional phone companies that were once part of AT&T), and upstarts like Sprint further eroded the company's position. For AT&T, it took more than a decade to begin regaining some of its lost market share.

What took it so long?

It required a number of mergers and, more important, the replacement of its operational leadership with a new group of strategic leaders. Once that transition was completed, the company began to grow once more.

Operational leadership, in contrast, was sorely lacking at big Wall Street firms like Lehman Brothers. The company was top heavy with a group of well-trained, high-IQ strategic thinkers who worked closely with Dick Fuld, the firm's chairman and CEO. Over time, Lehman grew, expanding its reach from the United States to Europe, Asia, and finally the Middle East. It won a large share of the world's securitized mortgage business and the world's trade in derivative products.

But while the firm was long on strategic vision, it was short on operational leadership. To win and keep its mortgage business, the firm began to borrow heavily, eventually borrowing as much as forty-four dollars for each one dollar of its own capital. Lehman's eleven-member board of directors (whose average age was sixty-eight) was heavily weighted with strategic leaders and nearly bereft of operational leaders. Whereas I have nothing against sixty-eight-year-old board members, the question is whether they are up to date. A financial expert in 1990 may find that many of his or her skills are out of date today with the plethora of new financial products being traded in the markets. As a result, the board watched, and applauded, each movement of the wrong needle. Increases in revenue and profits were applauded, while increases in risks were ignored. As a result, Lehman, like many other firms on Wall Street in the early 2000s, grew itself into oblivion.

Different types of leaders are required at different times in a firm's life. And just as organizations tend to cling too long to outmoded corporate and organizational structures, they also cling too long to the wrong type of leader. Organizations need to assess their challenges and then staff themselves accordingly. During times of cutthroat competition, it's wise to weight more heavily any advice that comes from a firm's strategic leadership. At other times, guidance coming from an organization's operational leadership needs to be more heavily weighted. But sometimes you need to weight each type of leadership equally.

In addition, Maccoby suggests another type of leadership role, which he calls *bridge builder.* In the United States, bridge builders are not always considered leaders. These are people who connect people together, transfer knowledge and information, make introductions, and help others achieve their goals. Venture capitalists, for example, are bridge builders. They raise capital and invest it on behalf of their partners in a process designed to enable others (strategic and operational leaders) to achieve their dreams.

By providing capital to Steve Jobs and Steve Wozniak, Apple's cofounders, the pioneering venture capitalist Arthur Rock served as a bridge builder. He did the same when he provided start-up capital to the founders of Fairchild Semiconductor, Intel, Teledyne, and Scientific Data Systems. Rock and other venture capitalists bring people together. But it's rarely their own dreams or their own strategies that they are pursuing. Instead, they connect people together to make things happen.

Bridge-building leaders are extremely important within organizations as well. As previously mentioned, the work of Robert Kelly and Janet Caplan, and their study of Bell Labs, shows that the ability to create networks, work laterally, and bring together teams is a vital component in any team's success. Kelly and Caplan's work suggests that bridge builders working closely with strategic and operational leaders create an almost unstoppable force for leadership and change. Bridge builders are also very good at creating alliances between companies and individuals.

How important is bridge building? Bill Clinton, when running for president of the United States, was reported to have a list containing fifty thousand contacts. Each of these people, if called by Clinton or one of his aides, could call another person, who in turn could call someone else. Think how much money, time, and effort fifty thousand "friends of Bill" could have contributed to Clinton's presidential campaign. Both George W. Bush and Barack Obama learned from Clinton's hyperactive bridge-building techniques.

BRINGING TOGETHER THE THREE LEADERSHIP ROLES

All three leadership roles—strategic, operational, and bridge building—are vital to creating a common purpose organization. Setting a goal (strategic leadership), making certain everything is being done that is needed to reach that goal (operational leadership), and ensuring that everyone is working together to achieve the same aims (bridge-building leadership) are essential to the success of any endeavor.

In truth, although these designations make a lot of sense, there are no absolutes. By that I mean, there is no job or person who is exclusively strategic. Nor is there any role within an organization that is only operational or bridge building. In reality, these three designations blend together, in people and in organizations, with certain traits more pronounced than others.

In the old days, and by that I mean the 1990s, it was thought that people were innately strategic, which meant they were ill suited for operational or bridge-building roles. This view was based on the belief that each type of leader thought differently and that the mental furniture of an operational leader, for example, was so different from that of a bridge builder or strategic leader that no amount of training would suffice to turn one type of leader into another. Certainly people have strengths and weaknesses, but I do not believe that excellence at one form of leadership means failure at another.

One thoughtful student of leadership, Elliot Jacques, a Canadian psychoanalyst and researcher into organizational behavior, thought that the critical factor that determined what type of leadership role a person could assume had to do with how far into the future that person could think. According to Jacques, how far into the future we can think is hardwired into us.

Jacques thought that to be a successful CEO of a large company, a candidate had to be able to think strategically approximately twenty years ahead. That's because big companies like IBM, GE, Toyota, and Intel, which operate in five- to ten-year investment cycles, require leaders who can think beyond that time frame to stay ahead of the competition. If you are investing in a chip fabrication plant with a useful life span of ten to fifteen years, you need to think beyond the useful life of that plant as soon as you break ground if your company is to stay ahead.

While being able to think into the future might be necessary if you are a CEO planning long-term strategy, it can get in the way if you are a salesperson. To be a successful salesperson, Jacques argued, you need to think only a few days, or perhaps a few

---

Time Frames of Leadership

- Warren Buffett: Forever (always buy, rarely sell companies)
- Fortune 500 CEO: Twenty years (build, buy, and sell companies)
- Chief of technology: Ten years (from lab to implementation)
- Sales director: One year (annual bonus period)
- Salesperson: Four weeks to three months (quotas)
- Director of cashiers: One day (tallying of the accounts)
- Cashier: Break-to-break

---

weeks, into the future. Any time frame longer than that can actually derail you.

Jobs fall roughly along a bell-shape curve, with only a few of them requiring a twenty-year time horizon and another few requiring a time horizon of hours or days. The vast array of jobs clusters in the middle, where the time horizon ranges from one to about five years. Doctors, especially emergency room physicians, work in very short time horizons of minutes, hours, or days. Journalists might work in time frames of days or weeks. Lawyers might work in time frames of months or a year or two, and road-building civil engineers might work in time horizons of two to five years. Against this time-based overlay, there are the strategic, operational, and bridge-building roles.

Jacques did not believe that the ability to think into the future could not be learned. He thought it was innate. For that reason, he believed, a great salesperson might fail if promoted to become CEO, and someone with the potential to become a big-company CEO might never get there if he or she had to rise up through sales, which emphasizes short-term thinking.

Since Jacques did his pioneering work in the 1970s and 1980s, it has become apparent that people are far more adaptable than

Jacques thought. And while they may have a specific time frame in which they feel most comfortable, they can learn to think further into the future or closer in, depending on their assignment.

Not only that, but strategic thinkers can learn organizational and bridge-building roles, although they might feel more comfortable in one role over another. The point is that people are far more adaptable than we otherwise thought.

LEADERSHIP TRAINING

I am a big believer in the need for leadership at all levels. Strategic, operational, and bridge-building leadership roles are all critical to the smooth functioning of organizations. And with the right training, people can learn the skills of each type of leadership role to add it to their repertoire of skills. Working with a deck of specially designed "networking cards," organizational development specialist Karen Warner helps operational and strategic leaders develop bridge-building skills. Working with bridge builders and operational leaders, Frank Cespedes, a former Harvard Business School professor, helps these individuals develop a larger, more future-oriented and strategic view. In addition, many schools, training centers, and workshops help people become better at operational pursuits.

The point is that while each of us has a leadership area where we're most comfortable, there are ways to develop the other types of leadership skills. We can develop new skills and add to our repertoire of effective leadership behavior.

Chapter Eleven

DIFFERENT STROKES FOR DIFFERENT GENERATIONS

THE NEWEST GENERATIONS

Since the time of Socrates and perhaps even before, people have been complaining about each new generation of workers and their proclivities. As a baby boomer, I can attest to the fact that we received our share of lumps, like Gen X's and Y's are receiving now. First, we boomers were scolded by our parents for not conforming to the standards of the time when we entered the labor market in the late 1960s and 1970s. Now we are being scolded again, this time by our kids, for remaining in the labor market too long and blocking their progress! Boomers were a phenomenon simply because of the size of the generation—a demographic pig swallowed and making its way through a python, we were delicately informed. And while today's Gen X is far smaller than the boomers, and Gen Y is larger than the Xers (they're sometimes called the echo boom or the millennials), both are different from the boomers and from each other. (While this topic in literature and the media seems ubiquitous of late, I was first introduced to these generational differences at work by Jay Conger, a professor at the University of Southern California working with Warren Bennis.)

There are a number of truisms about Gen X and Y. Both generations are probably more technologically literate than any previous generation. Both are more group oriented than the boomers, and this is especially true of the Y's, who can't seem to go anywhere without a posse.

They also have shorter attention spans and are adept at multitasking. Both generations tend to be idealistic and cause oriented, though the Y's are more so than the X's, who have a healthy appreciation of money.

Members of Gen Y, more than Gen X, do not want to work for organizations whose missions they do not share, whose business practices they do not like, and whose products are not socially and environmentally conscious. Gen X and Y tend to be less greedy than the boomers, but this can change. After all, the boomers were thought to be antimaterialistic, spiritual, and idealistic too.

Both Gen X and Gen Y tend to be more egalitarian than previous generations with regard to issues like gender, race, ethnic background, and sexual orientation. To their critics, they are the "whatever" generations. To their adherents, they are a bright new hope.

Taken together, it seems that younger workers, especially Gen Y workers, are wired for common purpose leadership. A high level of respect for individuals and their differences is a good place to start. In addition, younger workers, especially knowledge workers, entered the workforce when the new employment compact was already in full force. They never knew a time when employment was anything but a consensual decision. Nor did they come of age when loyalty between employer and employee and employee and employer was anything but at will.

Generation X and Y have had their disappointments in the workplace. Gen X came of age during the dot-com bubble and saw firsthand how bubbles end. Gen X and Y both experienced the tragic events of 9/11, with their impact on the psyche and the economy. Members of both generations experienced the run-up in housing prices, which kept them out of the market, and (if they were able to buy) also experienced the collapse of the housing and credit markets. Both generations were in the workforce during the steepest economic downturn since the Great Depression.

On the positive side, Gen X and Y voted overwhelmingly for the first African American president, Barack Obama, and saw their efforts at the polls rewarded by Obama's victory. With that win, Gen X and Gen Y began to understand the power of politics.

Gen X and Y really are different. John Tyson, chairman and CEO of Tyson Foods, one of the world's largest food companies, said that younger workers need more variety in their careers than their parents did if companies are to retain them. Part of the reason, said Tyson, is that the younger leaders grew up with far more choices, not to mention distractions, than their parents did. Unlike their parents, younger workers grew up with computers, video games, cell phones, and TV—sometimes with all of these items in use at once. Many had a host of planned activities in addition, like sports and after-school programs. As a result, younger workers expect more variety and more stimulation, all of it squeezed into shorter time frames.

To Tyson, that means younger people have to be made to feel that they're not caught in a rut: "These people need to know that it's okay to have outside interests. That they can play in a rock and roll band on the weekends." People in their twenties and thirties, and even a little older, don't necessarily do things sequentially, Tyson said. They do things in parallel. "You have to keep them interested."

INDIVIDUALITY

Common purpose leadership, at its most basic level, is about recognizing people as individuals. It doesn't matter if they are young or old, if they play in a band on weekends, if they are extremely intense and focused or if they multitask, if they're outdoors people or bookworms. Common purpose leadership begins with respect for individuals and their differences, and it goes on to celebrate their strengths. Since it is about individuals aligning themselves together to achieve goals, common purpose leadership is also about making up for each other's weaknesses.

As a boomer, my own theory about Gen X and Y is that they were raised differently from the boomers. Many were in day care or early childhood education classes, which gave them wide exposure to other children of all kinds when they were very young. Many of them have parents who were involved with their schools, after-school programs, and their lives. As a result, they grew up to be more sociable and group oriented than previous generations. This group orientation has been a big benefit to Gen X and Y, and it has made them adaptable. It has also made them conscious of the values expressed in each group of which they are a member. In addition, their early exposure to technology has made them highly literate and adept at multitasking.

When Admiral Cebrowski, head of force transformation at the Pentagon, invited me to a session with several generals, I recall one general talking to me at the break. He said the Pentagon had to redesign the controls of equipment such as tanks to make them more like video games so younger members of the armed services would feel at home. The inside of the tank, he explained, was also designed to be a multitasking environment. "I don't get it," the general admitted. "But I've watched my daughter as she does her home-work. She sits in her room reading a book with the TV on in the background, while she texts a friend and searches the Web with her laptop. If she didn't get such great grades, I'd object. But that's how they do it now. And if that's the case, then that's how we have to design our systems."

Gen X and Y Leaders

- They are more computer literate than their parents (though it's doubtful they can take apart a short-block Chevy engine like some boomers can).
- They are far more welcoming of diversity than older workers.
- Given when it entered the workforce—the recession of 1991, bursting of the dot-com bubble, 9/11, and the Enron scandal—Gen X has more than a healthy dose of skepticism.
- Gen Y has short attention spans and is frequently bored.
- Gen Y has a strong environmentalist bent.
- Gen X and Y require that the organizations they join have missions in which they believe.
- Gen X and Y are comfortable as part of a group.
- Gen X and Y are not as materialistic as baby boomers, though the boomers started out idealistic also.

This mix of high tech and high touch, to borrow the title of a book from decades ago, is how Gen X and Y leaders are organized. It's how they think. And it's how they lead. In addition, it seems, and it may be too early to tell, that Gen X and Y individuals are less materialistic than their parents. Many in Gen X and Y are interested in working in nonprofit organizations like Teach for America, at least at the beginning of their careers.

Members of Gen X and Y are uniquely qualified to lead. And yet because of accidents of fate and economics, they have not yet gotten the chance. Many were hired on Wall Street, only to be let go when the economy tanked, beginning in 2007. Others were working in traditional industries when the economy teetered.

For Gen X and Y individuals, says John Tyson, the career path has to "zigzag rather than go in a straight line." Young people, especially these young people, are used to change. As a result, leaders must set up programs to develop them that move them around the organization and have them interact with lots of different groups.

Gen X and Y think differently about work, because, said Tyson, "they saw their moms and dads get on a career trail and stay on it for thirty years. They also saw that it didn't quite work out and that their moms and dads were frustrated. And they also saw their moms and dads being happier when they were off work—you know, having a little barbecue on the weekends—than when they were working." These observations formed the basis of Gen X and Y's relationship to work. They don't want to get caught in a rut or trapped in a job without meaning to them. And they certainly don't want to create common purpose inside an organization that doesn't have a higher purpose.

In many ways, I believe, today's Gen X and Y individuals have a major role to play in the world.

Boomers are working longer. They are doing so not just because they failed to save enough to retire or lost large sums in the economic downturn. They are working longer because they are healthier and better educated than previous generations and because there are some significant leadership and labor shortages in certain sectors of the economy. Because boomers are remaining in the workforce longer, it is up to younger workers to remind their aging colleagues that there is more to life than a paycheck. Gen X and Y leaders are the perfect generation to rekindle the spark of youth and idealism in their gray-haired colleagues. They are suited to do this because of their openness to others (Gen Y is especially involved with their parents, who tended to be quite protective) and because of their embrace of diversity.

But Gen X and Y have their own destinies and can't spend their entire careers looking after a few million of their closest, albeit aged, peers. Even so, one of their aims is probably to make certain their own values of inclusiveness and idealism do not get left by the wayside. It is important for organizations to stand for more than the bottom line. And if members of the boomer generation have been derelict in this, it is up to members of subsequent generations to take up the challenge as an element of their leadership.

The question is, if they don't do it, who will?

BUSINESS AND LIFE

I have always argued that we make a big mistake when we think of business as a separate category from the rest of life. And today, with a wide array of technology that links us to our jobs at all hours of the day and night and almost no matter where we are in the world, it is difficult to make the case that work and life are separate. Work and life are, in fact, seamlessly integrated. And if we are unhappy in one, chances are we are unhappy in the other. For that reason, it is vital that we do not make leadership distinctions between work and life. Those values that we uphold when we are with family and friends should be the same ones we uphold when we are with the people with whom we make our living.

Organizations have rules, customs, and behaviors we employ to coordinate our activities in the pursuit of large goals. Organizations are not the desks in our offices, the computers on our desks, or the machines that stamp out parts. Organizations are us, in a way, and they codify and clarify the way we get things done.

Many years ago when I studied systems analysis and worked with philosopher of science Ervin Laszlo, we spent a lot of time thinking about organizations from a systems point of view. The conclusion we came to after years of discussion and debate was that values are not optional. They are, in fact, the way organizations operate. If an organization allows people to disrespect each other, then you cannot consider such behavior an anomaly. It is a value. If an organization tolerates buccaneering behavior, with irrationally high rates of leverage, these are its values. If it allows its executives to stay isolated from the real world so they fly on their private jets to a congressional hearing in search of a handout, then isolating the CEO from reality is an organizational value.

In its simplest terms, an organization's values are identical to the way it does business. There is no anomalous behavior, no lapse. What is tolerated within the organization is what the organization values. Values are expressions of behavior far more than they are words.

In many cases, the organizations for which we work express an entirely different set of values from the homes in which we live. And yet for the most part, we are far more accepting of work behaviors than of the types of behaviors we experience at home. In fact, if we have children, we usually spend hours teaching them not to perpetuate the types of behaviors we experience routinely at work.

Leaders must take it on themselves to make certain that the values their organizations express are the right ones. I say that because a further conclusion of my early study of systems was that values determine whether an organization will survive or fail.

In the run-up to the recession beginning in 2007, which saw the extinction of Bear Stearns and Lehman Brothers, the loss of independence of firms like Merrill Lynch, and the bankruptcy of firms like Chrysler and many others, none of these business and organizational problems were caused by any other factor than their (misguided) values and an inability, or reluctance, among leaders to change those values. Greed, carelessness, reckless behavior, insularity, and intransigence among certain groups of workers are far more deadly than power outages, soaring resource prices, and a fickle marketplace.

Values matter. And yet when you or I suggest that to leaders working within organizations, they do not always see it. Perhaps worse, they pretend to care about whether their organizational values are intact.

The task for leaders, real leaders, especially among those in Gen X and Y, is to unabashedly argue for the importance of values and against the fantasy that work and life are somehow different. The goal for leaders today must be to make certain that their organizations can persist into the future and flourish. And they must do it by making the case that values matter, and not just those related to competitiveness. All values matter: the positive ones and those that inhibit the survivability of the organization. Values, simply put, are "how we do things around here." For leaders, the challenge is to keep those values as shiny, new, and survival oriented as the latest computer on the floor or the latest design or process makeover.

Chapter Twelve

You Don't Have to Be Ruthless to Lead

Who Finishes First?

What's more important to the success of a company: competent leaders or nice leaders? If you ask me, competent people are not in short supply. Each year the nation's business schools turn out tens of thousands of graduates proficient in marketing, finance, human resource management, accounting, general management, strategy, and banking. Each year the nation's engineering schools turn out tens of thousands of graduates who understand building construction and can figure out how a tornado or fire will affect a warehouse. In addition, the insurance industry trains its own people to very high standards. And while brains, raw talent, education, and training matter, none of these factors on their own explains success. In my view, and in the view of William Baker, a professor at Columbia University who teaches about social intelligence, kindness, caring, and empathy are powerful factors for success.

If we go back to the work of Richard Boyatzis at Case Western Reserve University and consider his view that a great deal of work takes place within toxic, fear-laden environments and if we further consider his view that toxic organizations result in workers who are dispirited, unproductive, and frequently ill, then it should come as no surprise that kindness, empathy, and caring energize teams.

But, some might ask, don't kindness, empathy, and caring sound weak? How can you compete when you are nice? The answer is that kindness, empathy, and caring are powerful forces that lead to great results when they are mobilized. When leaders exhibit these types of emotions, they are clearing the air of the type of emotional toxicity that dulls focus and blunts productivity.

Caring is an important leadership tool no matter who the followers are. According to Colin Powell, who led the United States and its allies in the first Gulf War, "The day soldiers stop bringing you their problems is the day you have stopped leading them. They have either lost confidence that you can help them, or concluded you do not care. Either case is a failure of leadership." Powell's kind, empathic style doesn't mean the mission is compromised. Far from it. Powell was able to rout Saddam Hussein's forces, which were dug in after invading Kuwait, and force the dictator to surrender by using overwhelming force strategically deployed.

In spite of the fact that empathic leadership is powerful, men and women working in organizations are often too timid to try it. Instead they set a course and then expect others to follow it. Or they work as a group to set a course. Where they go wrong is that they don't pay enough attention to the fact that the other members of their team are people too and that people perform far better when they are well regarded.

This is not to say that some people demand too much. They do. And as Jean-René Fourtou said, people who demand too much, do not contribute, or are naysayers and negative will take every second of a leader's time if given the chance. To put it bluntly, these people should be dismissed. They are disruptive and counter-productive, and they diminish the output of others. Kind leaders need not be dumb leaders or pushovers.

What Great Leaders Do

- They make certain the mood of the organization is positive and accomplishment oriented.
- They remove toxic emotions from the organization not by being a Pollyanna but by focusing on the positive application of effort.
- They distinguish between chronically negative people and people who might engage in creative disagreements for the long-term good of the organization.
- If they fail at changing chronically negative people into people who are positive, they remove the negative people from their teams.

FM Global's leaders are kind, empathic, and caring. You see it in the way they interact in the lunch room, the way they hold meetings, the way they allow for each other's proclivities and foibles. They are individuals who work as a team, and they care how each other is doing.

But don't make the mistake of thinking that leaders who care are weak. They are not. In fact, kindness, empathy, and caring are actually far more likely to bring out people's strengths than their weaknesses. And because you care about your own team's members does not mean you are less of a competitor against your rivals. In fact, FM Global is a fierce competitor: everyone there does as much as they can to win new business and retain the business they have. What else would explain FM Global's 95 percent retention rate?

That shouldn't be so strange. People serving in the military form bonds that are so powerful they are willing to risk their lives for one another. They do it because they trained the same way, have the same mission, face the same perils, and were put in a position to watch each other's backs. This forms a strong interdependent relationship where one person's success and safety depends on the actions of another. Close relationships form and strong bonds are created when military personnel serve together.

These bonds, based on mutual caring and concern, are among the strongest bonds humans form. In conflict situations, it's not at all uncommon for one soldier to risk his or her life for another. Bonds between soldiers are sometimes stronger than those between soldiers and their families. And it's also not uncommon for soldiers to spend hours discussing their worries and concerns with each other. Far from being emotionally remote or cold or cut off, soldiers tend to be kind to each other and empathic as well. In today's military, leaders like General George Patton (called "Blood and Guts" by his World War II troops) are the rarity rather than the rule.

The best leaders are those who care deeply about the people on their teams. In fact, I suggest that one essential quality of a successful leader is to enjoy and be interested in people. And while this may be a controversial statement, given that Harvard's Abraham Zelaznik wrote in Harvard Business School case studies, as well as in the *Harvard Business Review,* that the best leaders are often people who are neurotic outsiders, I stand by my contention: the best leaders are people who love or at least enjoy and are interested in other people.

But let's not confuse success with leadership. I have known some misanthropic people who have been very successful. I have known investors, analysts, consultants, and serial acquirers who made many millions, and in some cases billions, of dollars and never cared for people. They were successes in business, and some were even moguls, but they were not leaders.

Why weren't they leaders? Because no one followed them unless they were paid to do so. And when they did follow them, they did so grudgingly and with a lot of nasty talk behind the mogul's back. The only purpose these misanthropic moguls shared was topping up their bank accounts. And when the funds or investment groups had a down year, their so-called loyal teammates deserted them.

There are many expedient relationships in life. And nothing is more disheartening than the "I laughed all the way to the bank" type of relationship where people joined an enterprise for no other reason than to put money in their pockets.

I have nothing against money. In fact, I'm quite partial to it. But when money is the only reason to join a company or work on a team, there is something sad about that relationship.

Work and life are not separate domains, and the rules that govern one ought to govern the other. I believe, as Boyatzis and others point out, that certain types of working relationships can be toxic. When that happens, the aims of the group are thwarted, and individuals can suffer. When people work only for money, the filter they use to choose their place of employment will not turn up toxicity as something to worry about. As a result, the sad truth is that mercenary-oriented people are very likely to end up in situations they abhor while failing to achieve the ends they so much desire.

SURVIVAL OF THE KINDEST

We tend to think that macho leaders—take-charge alpha men and women—are the most effective people at getting things done. But it is not always the case. In fact, it may only rarely be the case. It turns out that the people who are the most effective leaders are those who bring out the best in others. They are effective because the purpose of an organization is to coordinate the efforts of individuals so they can achieve goals that are beyond the capacity of an individual to accomplish alone. As a result, it stands to reason that the best leaders, the most effective leaders, are people who can motivate and guide others to do their best. These leaders create a work and organizational environment where high performance is the norm. They do it, as Joe Rice does at CD&R, through a mix of humility, clear communications, a common language, and hands-on coaching in an environment of mutual respect. Great leaders are people who help others do their best. And by doing so, they create an organizational environment that is positive, upbeat, even happy.

One such leader, Robert Maxson, an educator who led several very large institutions of higher learning, such as the University of Las Vegas, with twenty-eight thousand students, and California State University, Long Beach, with thirty-eight thousand students, and is now president of Sierra Nevada College, at Lake Tahoe, believes that happiness is an important element in leadership. According to Maxson, happiness is important because it liberates individuals' energy and helps them engage with life. "Happiness is a decision," Maxson said. "If you decide to be happy, then you increase your ability to achieve."

Prior to the work of Richard Boyatzis, Maxson's perspective might have been interesting but without a basis in fact. But since the advent of Boyatzis's work, the reason that empathy, kindness, caring, and even happiness are powerful leadership tools is suddenly evident: they help people lead because they are antidotes to a toxic workplace.

What all this means is that one primary, and usually overlooked, job of leaders is to prevent the buildup of organizational toxins. Leaders need to pay a great deal of attention to the emotional climate of the workplace, not as nice to have but as essential to the workplace.

Paradoxically leaders must be rather brutal at how they do this. If people are negative consistently, even in the face of good news and good results, they need to be counseled and coached, and if neither approaches works, they need to be removed from the organization. Ramit Varma and Jake Neuberg, founders of the fast-growing educational company Revolution Prep, understand this. They know that you can't build a positive, expansive company with negative people.

But far too often we're too permissive. Evaluations don't always take into account a team member's attitude, and when they do, the weightings are usually pretty low. But attitude matters. And as the example of Men's Warehouse shows, individual performance is not always a good indicator of group performance. Negative, back-biting, morale-destroying team members may be clever enough to conceal their intentions and may even have individual statistics, such as sales, that camouflage the damage they have done to the overall organization.

I once had an individual work for me who was an excellent worker and team member—on the surface. He appeared thoughtful, concerned, and caring. He sent out witty Christmas cards and birthday cards to everyone on the team. He was well trained and well educated, and on the surface he was an outstanding performer. But he also had a tendency, behind my back, to focus on the negative in ways that destroyed morale. He often spoke negatively of our firm (I won't say which one), and he criticized the leadership. He was nostalgic for the good old days and, I was told, reminded people frequently that even our best efforts could not compare to what was done in the past. And yet there was nothing tangible I could point to, even though my colleagues and fellow team members from time to time told me that things this individual said made them un-comfortable, and even demoralized them.

Then one of the firm's controllers asked me to review with her some charges this individual had expensed. It was amazing! Together we looked through page after page of expenses that were bogus, inflated, or incorrect. As we peered into the matter further, we learned that most likely there were also kickbacks between this individual and some of our suppliers. Needless to say, when confronted, the individual had an explanation for every charge. But when further study was undertaken, it turned out that none of his explanations were correct. He was terminated on the spot.

I'm not suggesting that every negative individual is stealing from the organization. But I am suggesting that when people are unhappy and a good-faith effort is made to address their concerns and give them counsel, then they are probably doing far more damage to the organization than they are helping it.

I once consulted to a financial services firm that had a stellar reputation and was in the process of trying to select the successor to the chief executive. In a highly competitive, high-stakes field like this, several individuals were competing to succeed the CEO. A succession committee was organized.

The reputation one fellow had was that he was a brilliant deal maker—a genius, in fact—who was so much smarter than anyone else that he had no patience for them. As a result, he was often abrupt and many times very disrespectful of younger people and even of his peers. Although he was often intimidating, he had some strong supporters on the committee who thought that if his rough edges were smoothed out, he'd be a great leader.

The first time I interviewed the candidate to see if he was a good fit to succeed the CEO, he didn't show up for the appointment. He simply blew me off. In the world of deal making, deals take precedence over interviews, so I was not concerned.

The second time I went to see him, he was very confrontational. "Why do we need you?" he demanded. "We can make our own decisions. You just cost us money. It's not a good use of anybody's money or time."

I listened to this fellow and was immediately put on the defensive. Not only was he aggressive and highly combative, he was downright rude. In fact, I left the meeting surprised that he was even in the running for the top job.

"You don't get it," a member of the succession committee told me. "He's a genius. He cuts deals that have returned to us a profit when other firms would have lost money. He has finance in his blood and bones."

Even so, I told this member of the succession committee I still didn't think the candidate in question was the right fit. I thought, in fact, that he might even tear up the firm given his demeanor and capacity to intimidate.

I spent more than a month talking with people in the firm and discussing all of the issues relating to succession at length. And in the end, the firm listened to my counsel and picked a leader who was far less aggressive; more diplomatic, kind, and caring and, some might say, a point or two less brilliant than the other candidate.

As a result of the decision, the abrasive deal maker announced he had decided to leave the firm to start his own company. He stormed out of the office and opened up a new company across the street. Within days, he had raised more than $1 billion to get his enterprise off the ground. When that happened, one member of the succession committee expressed to me his view that perhaps the committee had made the wrong choice.

But, not unexpectedly, the new company became a revolving door for talent. Great people were hired, but they didn't last long. Pretty soon, the new firm developed a reputation as a place that paid well but didn't treat people well. In an odd paradox, the firm, which was headed by a genius, ended up being staffed by second-raters who were there only for the money. Two years later, the firm had gone out of business.

LEADING WITH THE HEART

The leaders I most admire at all levels are those who care about people and lead with their hearts. They are men and women who know that one of their jobs is to rid their team, and their organization, of negativity. And they understand the massive difference between creating an environment where creative disagreement is fostered, in pursuit of the best solution, and allowing an environment to develop where negativity builds up and becomes toxic.

Chapter Thirteen

Ideas Matter

Thought Leadership

Without thought leadership, which is to say without good, workable ideas, no leader is likely to accomplish very much. Leadership is not like golf or tennis, with most of an individual's success accounted for by the actions of the wrists. Real leadership is thought leadership. Common purpose begins with good ideas and carries them forward. Over time, it replenishes tired ideas with new ones. When an organization is bereft of new ideas, its life and longevity are in danger. And yet far too often, I have seen leaders, especially leaders at the top, fail to replenish their ideas.

To paraphrase former Harvard professor and statesman Henry Kissinger, prior to assuming office, an individual is a creator of intellectual capital. After assuming office, that individual tends to become a consumer of intellectual capital. That's a pity. At no other time in an executive's career are ideas more important than when he or she is in a leadership role.

Over the years, whenever I interviewed CEOs or other top leaders, I always asked what they were reading. The question usually caught them by surprise. Great leaders are constantly reading, constantly replenishing their intellectual capital, constantly generating and developing new ideas. Poor leaders—those who fail at generating common purpose—are usually idea free.

Many thoughtful leaders are devotees of Peter Drucker or Michael Porter. Others read C. K. Prahalad or Jim Kouzes and Barry Posner. There are many thought leaders who can help leaders generate new ideas. Some leaders I interviewed have read their favorite business and organizational authors numerous times. Others told me they were devotees of the *Harvard Business Review* or some other august publication in print or on the Web. And still others point to a long list of technical publications or professionally oriented materials. Sadly, however, I've observed that the percentage of leaders who have continued to replenish their intellectual resources are in the minority.

Not every publication you read has to be about your business or organizational mission. Many leaders tell me that they are devotees of biographies. They indicate their love of American or European history and argue that reading about Churchill or Adams or Truman—or any other leader, for that matter—provides them with insights they use every day. (One very honest exception to that was George M. C. Fisher, who, when he was chairman and CEO of Kodak, told me that as a mathematician, he had never read a management book. He was honest and forthright. He said that he based his decisions about management on what he thought was right and by doing a lot of analysis of each situation.)

I certainly agree that reading biographies is very helpful to anyone assuming a leadership role at any level in an organization—if they really read what they say they do, that is. The problem is that too many leaders are faking it. They say they read about Churchill or Eisenhower or FDR, but in reality they are doing nothing of the sort. In fact, when I interviewed leaders and asked them what they were reading, I always was skeptical when they mentioned some old biography of Churchill. It was just too much of a cliché.

Now I'm not saying that there's no value to reading about the life of Churchill. There is. He was a great leader who was counted out more than once. It's just that CEOs and other leaders should be reading much more widely. Today's problems might be great and small, but they are hardly new. Hannibal, who led his men and his elephants up the Iberian coast and then down into Italy through a passageway in the Alps, had logistical issues, not to mention morale issues, that would confound any leader today. Napoleon Bonaparte was a consummate strategist. Alexander Hamilton was one of the world's most prescient bankers. The point is that many of the problems over which we struggle have been met before and bested. We need not pursue those problems alone. Rather than viewing reading as a burden, it is a help.

Another problem leaders have with thought leadership is that they don't really understand why they need to be thought leaders. They don't understand the link between ideas and competitiveness. They don't understand the importance of innovation.

Organizations, and the people who lead them, can't fake ideas. They either have winning strategies or they don't. They are either innovative or they are not. And if they're not, they have an obligation to do whatever they can to seek out ideas and disseminate them throughout their organization. They also have a responsibility to create an environment in which new ideas and innovations feel at home. They need to make everyone on their team understand that leadership is thought leadership at every level.

This means that today's leaders have an added responsibility. Rather than simply rallying the team, they need to create an environment where ideas matter. Maintaining leadership means becoming a thought leader.

GROWING IDEAS

Many large companies are involved with organizations that stress ideas. The top people in the organization attend sessions of the World Economic Forum, the Milken Institute Global Conference, the Aspen Ideas Fest, and TED, among other conferences. In some cases, companies spend many thousands of dollars for their people to attend these meetings.

But if you sit down and discuss the real reason for attending these forums and conferences, many CEO-level leaders will tell you they go for the networking.

I have nothing against networking. It's essential to the way we conduct business. But the leader who stands outside the seminar room hoping to meet other luminaries isn't doing much for his or her organization's learning needs. Just as bad, senior-level leaders who go to high-level meetings usually fail to share what they learn with other members of their teams or with their organizations as a whole. They sit in lectures or participate on panels and rarely summarize what they learned. They may grow and gain insight from attending these sessions, but no one else will. To be effective, knowledge must be communicated widely within the organization.

COMMUNICATING KNOWLEDGE

Ideas must be transmitted if they are to make a difference. The more widely they are disseminated, the more powerful their effect. And yet most organizations do a pretty poor job at transmitting what they know so others can use it.

When I was an alliance partner at Booz & Co. (then called Booz, Allen & Hamilton), I started a magazine called *strategy+business*. The point of the magazine was to showcase the firm's thought leadership and gather up thought leaders from around the world to capture their ideas and share them with clients. The magazine was a big hit, and it continues to dazzle people with its breadth and depth. It was also the place where the words *thought leadership* were used for the first time to designate someone whose ideas merited attention.

But as we were getting the publication off the ground and clients were beginning to read it, it became apparent to me that we had one large group of people who were in the dark with regard to the ideas contained in the publication: the employees and partners of Booz & Co!

What do you do when you publish a magazine containing some of the best ideas in business and members of your own firm don't read it? How do you make them aware of the importance of ideas? Our solution, with my consulting firm patron's blessings, was to hop on planes and fly around the world to nearly every Booz & Co. office to personally brief people on how to read the magazine, use the magazine with clients, and write for the magazine. In other words, I conducted a thought leadership tutorial.

Standing in front of a group of consultants (usually at lunchtime) was a lot of fun. I showed the publication and took them through the roster of people who had written for it. I pointed out where the magazine broke new ground. And I explained to them why we interviewed the people we did.

These presentation were always spirited. They began with overviews of the publication but soon erupted into arguments about the ideas the magazine contained. As the focus shifted from talking about the magazine to arguing about ideas, my role changed from presenter to facilitator.

I tried to make this shift as seamless as possible. At these meetings, I moderated arguments regarding C. K. Prahalad's ideas about strategy, the importance of knowledge management, how Harley-Davidson built its brand, what the Web was doing to commerce, and how the Grateful Dead could be such a successful band despite never having a single number one hit.

What I learned from these trips to Booz & Co.'s offices was how much people loved to think about ideas. I also learned how much the consultants liked thinking on behalf of their clients. And when we brought consultants and clients together and turned them loose on a problem, the results were nothing less than magnificent.

In one of those breakfast sessions, which we held in New York, I brought together the manager of a Harley-Davidson dealership outside Boston, Steven Greyser, a professor of marketing at the Harvard Business School, and Sam Hill, Booz's chief marketing officer. About a hundred people attended the breakfast. The question I asked the panel to address was how to reach a market in which demographics are very different, as they are with Harley, which is selling to members of the Hells Angels motorcycle gang, on the one hand, and doctors, lawyers, and other professionals, on the other. The interactions among the panelists were fascinating, and the questions from the attendees were perceptive. But what really got people's attention was when the store manager said his piece. After all, he was the guy who worked with the customers and had to juggle the needs of someone who works two months to buy a custom fender and someone who buys an entire motorcycle for cash. What he said, to be brief, was that the commonality that cut across income groups was the need for freedom. When someone walked into his showroom, his job was not just to sell motorcycles but to sell freedom. His job was to sell freedom from nine-to-five jobs, freedom from worry, freedom from fear, freedom from drudgery. It wasn't an object he was selling but a lifestyle and a dream.

In addition to going around the world talking about ideas, I developed a modest prize (dinner for two) that was awarded each month to the person at the firm who found a copy of the magazine in the most interesting place. I used the idea of a monthly prize to get people to build internal awareness for the magazine and its ideas, and to help people understand that the magazine was being read by clients.

People found the magazine in a number of interesting places: in CEOs' offices, private aviation airports, the bathroom of a former professor's home, an airport lounge, the seat back of a commercial jet, and as a prop in a Jim Carrey movie. The more we publicized the contest, the more people paid attention to the magazine.

For a consulting firm like Booz & Co., the power of ideas is a given. Firms like that think for a living, and publishing a magazine for clients and employees is a good way to educate people on the importance of ideas.

Ideas are important to other types of organizations in addition to consulting firms, and several companies I worked with understood this point. Over the years, Whirlpool and HP published their own management journals. A number of firms I've worked with bring in speakers on a regular basis to push their thinking and keep them fresh.

One pharmaceutical firm I know brought in a freedom fighter to its New Jersey headquarters who was a member of the African National Congress and had fought alongside Nelson Mandela. The pharmaceutical company was in the drug discovery business and thought that spending a day with someone who had waged a life-and-death campaign against social and political injustice would help them understand their own quest to discover new medications.

Each time organizations bring in thought leaders to discuss topics that are relevant to their own activities, they create a tangible benefit for the firm. People's sights are raised, and they are reminded that there is more than one way to get things done and that ideas matter.

INNOVATION LEADERS

Ideas are especially important in today's highly competitive economy because the surest way to succeed is by out-innovating your rivals. Innovation is the application of creativity to solve problems and create lasting advantage. But I use the world *lasting* advisedly, because advantage doesn't last long in a world where competition comes from all quarters. Lasting advantage in today's environment depends on the industry. As a result, innovation itself has changed. Instead of something an organization does every once in a while, it now must do it continuously.

If leaders are to be innovative, they must continuously develop new ideas. Nothing should be off-limits, and everything must be approached with an innovative eye.

Tom Kelley, chairman and CEO of IDEO, a firm that specializes in innovation and has won numerous awards for its designs and inventions, said that innovation is the responsibility of both the individual and the group. A person working in an organization might have a great idea for a new product or service. But then what? Chances are that person must interact with others to turn that idea into something tangible and lasting. The team must make certain the new idea really is new, it works, and it can be applied. In other words, although an individual may have a brainstorm that leads to something new, it's up to the team to turn that brainstorm into something real.

For leaders, this creates a very important dynamic. First, leaders must make it clear that the organization is actually looking for something new. That's not as easy as it sounds. Many people become quite skeptical when they hear that the company has *now* decided to become an innovator. As a result, leaders are often required to convince members of their team that this time the organization means business. To do that, leaders must be armed with their new ideas and with anecdotes and stories that show that the organization values innovation. To do that, leaders must demonstrate that they are enthusiastic about innovation. Then when somebody comes up with a great idea, the leader must act to make certain that if the idea is good (and not all of them are), the organization is willing to put resources behind it.

"Sometimes the initial idea can be big, but it still might account for only 1 percent of the work," said Kelley. "The other

99 percent has to be done by the team. It's that team of people who figure out how to make the product, how to sell it, how to make sure it doesn't break, how to introduce it, how to get it into distribution. So innovation is pretty collaborative."

What's true for a product is also true for a service. An insight might pop out of one person's mind, but it must be developed by the team. What that means is that thought leadership is also thought management. The leader, after removing all of the organization's blockages, must make certain that the organization really does support innovation.

This takes courage. Many organizations say they are innovators but are afraid to commit resources to that end. The CEO or someone else writes a memo or circulates an e-mail or makes it known in some other way that "we are an innovation-driven organization." And yet nothing could be further from the truth. When most organizations come in contact with a new idea, their first instinct is to stamp it out.

For that reason, thought leadership is one of the most important aspects of leadership in general. To compete in the future, organizations must commit themselves to almost continuous change. Thought leaders must be courageous, but they are also targets. They are the ones who want to (1) "spend all that money," (2) "commit the firm to an untested path," (3) "waste our time," or (4) "take us on wild goose chases." As a result, each new idea is likely to face opposition no matter how publicly the organization is committed to innovation.

I speak about this from experience. At PricewaterhouseCoopers, my title was "global lead partner for thought leadership and innovation." And while I had one of the world's greatest (and longest) titles, I learned the hard way how difficult it was to get people to change their ways.

But not everyone was opposed to new ideas. I also learned at PwC that change and new ideas have some natural allies, especially young people, and to make certain that when it comes to thought leadership, new ideas, and innovation, it is important to mix senior people with young people. Even if you are managing a team that includes the chairman and CEO (both typically with more than a few gray hairs), be sure to include some young people on the team. Not only do they add youthful energy, but they haven't been brainwashed into thinking "this is the way we do things around there." They are open. Innovation requires a mix of seasoned people and young leaders if it is to work.

THINKING DIFFERENTLY

From the mid-1990s through 2004, I ran Microsoft's annual CEO Summit. Each year, Microsoft invited about 120 CEOs from around the world to spend a day and a half at the Microsoft campus, followed by a reception and dinner at Bill Gates's fascinating, art-filled home.

For the first few years, our approach to the summit was to bring in speakers from around the world who could hold forth on topics of interest to CEOs. CEOs came to network, visit the campus, meet Bill Gates and see his home, and learn about technology and business.

These sessions were always fascinating. Some of the world's best business thinkers spoke at the summit: Nicholas Negroponte, head of MIT's Media Lab; Clayton Christensen, the Harvard professor who gave us the idea of disruptive technology; Faith Popcorn, the marketing expert; and many others. Each of these sessions with a business guru was preceded by a session led by Gates or another Microsoft employee on the future of technology.

No one complained about the program. In fact, the CEOs seemed to like what we did. But one year we tried something new. Rather than fill the afternoon with outside speakers, we called on the CEOs themselves to contribute. This was not as risky as it might sound. Most of the guests were household names—Fortune 500 CEOs. And if they didn't know each other before the summit, they had at least heard about each other and perhaps even done deals with each other. There were also luminaries like Warren Buffett, who has opinions about almost everything relating to business, and the Microsoft team, composed of Bill Gates, Steve Ballmer, and several other senior Microsoft employees.

Interestingly, the more we involved the CEOs in the program, the more they seemed to enjoy it and learn from it. We once did a session on business-to-business Web commerce with the chairmen/ CEOs of Boeing, GM, and PricewaterhouseCoopers. During the discussion period, after each CEO made his case, there were comments from Gates and other business leaders.

It turned out that the assembled leaders learned a lot from their peers. They listened intently, did not interrupt, and tried out their hypotheses on each other. It was an exciting program to facilitate and to watch.

From these sessions, it struck me that it's not mandatory that you have all the answers when you try to solve an organizational or business problem. Skin in the game counts for a lot. So do preparation, goodwill, and a willingness to take intellectual risks. What it all adds up to is authenticity. CEOs listened to each other because they were authentic in their perspectives and because they cared about the problem they were trying to solve. The fact that they lacked Ph.D.s, had never conducted research, or had never written an article or a book was far less important than that they were authentic leaders.

The critical piece in making these sessions work, it turned out, was not just making certain that the CEOs were well prepared. It was also making certain that they were talking about an issue with which they were personally involved. When CEOs did their homework, when they read the latest papers, and when the issue affected them personally, they became as masterful as the gurus in presenting their ideas.

The point I am making is that ideas should not be viewed as the sole possession of consultants, academics, and gurus. Because they

are an important source of competitive advantage, ideas are everyone's business in an organization. As a result, leaders should search
for new ideas the way a shark searches for food: relentlessly, tirelessly,
and ruthlessly.

Microsoft's high-level CEO Summit is not the only game in
town. There are many different types of thought leadership sessions
that are valuable to companies. Some of these are routinely done,
and others are interesting one-offs. But all of them are important and
highly rated by the people in attendance.

I have been to meetings at an insurance company based in New
York where a group of midlevel managers brought in a different
speaker every other week to discuss ideas the company should be
thinking about, especially with regard to risk.

At a Boston-based advertising and PR company, Brodeur
Partners, an Omnicom Company, most staff members participate
in regular brown-bag lunches for clients where they talk about ideas.
Brodeur also has a board of thought leaders that it brings in once or
twice a year to talk about consumer trends and how they are affecting
the market.

At Fidelity Investments, I participated in a monthly thought
leadership session put on for fund managers and focusing on market
trends. The fund manager who led the sessions, Neal Miller, was
interested mostly in lateral interactions (how one event links to
another event in unexpected ways). Miller explained it to me by
saying that on a visit to a factory in which he was thinking of investing,
he noticed that many of the production workers wore so-called
designer jeans. This told him that despite their high prices, these
jeans went mostly on the, ah, derrières, of working-class people, not
jet-setting executives. As a result, he realized the companies producing
these products were probably much more sensitive to the ups and
downs of the business cycle than, say, producers of true luxury goods,
like France's Hermès. This insight was not linear, he said, but lateral.
And it paid off in Miller's investments.

One speaker who came to this group explained how in the go-go 1990s, when money was plentiful and many people became rich, two interesting trends occurred simultaneously. The first was the widespread use of the lighthouse as a corporate and business symbol. The other was the astounding increase in sales for the so-called Wonderbra. These two trends, the expert said, indicated the exuberance of those times.

I have participated in quarterly brainstorming sessions at a major global bank to discuss its businesses and how it can position itself for the future. I have been invited to a two-day meeting in London at an energy company to discuss trends affecting world energy demand. And I have watched as a large Japanese automaker brought in customers for a day to discuss what they liked and didn't like about its cars.

In each of these instances, and in many more, I have seen how individuals working inside organizations have wrestled with ideas on a deep and serious level in an effort to improve their companies and stretch their minds. And in each instance, attendance at these sessions was not only rated as a perk—a benefit of working at the company—but was also viewed as critical to the way each firm's leaders did their jobs. In each of these instances, it was heartening to see that a number of very large organizations put their faith in ideas and are not afraid to debate and discuss issues of importance. And with only one exception, it came as no surprise to me that each of the companies seriously pursuing thought leadership strategies was a leader in its business and its sector.

Ideas do more than matter; they are competitive differentiators. Companies that embrace thought leadership win because they are fearless when it comes to assessing their strengths and weaknesses. And even more important, companies that embrace thought leadership win because they recognize that the world is not static. Rather, they understand that it is constantly changing and that in order for them to keep pace, they must do what Socrates said everybody should do: question all assumptions.

TRUE LEADERSHIP

Leadership is about working with your team to achieve goals. A great deal of the time those goals are stretch goals and not easy to achieve. Progress requires hard work and dedication. It takes strategy and a thoughtful analysis of all of the tactics that are available. Good leadership requires an active mind.

What this means is that one of the worst mistakes a leader can make is to become intellectually lazy. Real leaders need to take in enormous amounts of information and knowledge and to process what they take in from the vantage point of their team and from the point of view of their organization and its mission. They must pore over newspapers, magazines, and books. They must review what's on the Web. Leaders must spend a lot of time searching for ideas.

It may sound like a truism, but learning organizations must make learning available to everyone who works there—and that can take many forms, from office book clubs to budgets for seminars and conferences to paying for advanced degrees.

Thought leadership is not an add-on; it should be part of every firm's strategies. And although a lot of companies have adopted the words, few firms have really embraced them. Thought leadership is a powerful form of leadership, but it is not an easy form. To be successful, companies must be open enough and transparent enough to question everything.

EPILOGUE:
THE FUTURE OF LEADERSHIP

Leadership is evolving. How could that not be the case? Organizations are flatter, and leaders operating within those organizations have had to adapt. Rather than being handed an organization chart of the company's hierarchy and a career plotting map, newly hired employees at any large organization are handed a question mark. Where does the leadership want the company want to go? How likely are their chances of getting it there? Are they trustworthy? Ethical? Is this organization a positive place to work, or is it toxic? Will the company remain independent, or might it be acquired? Will it be protected by the government (and perhaps be allowed to languish and rot), or will it be forced to compete with tough, foreign rivals in a battle whose outcome is very much in doubt? Will the new employee's skills and knowledge be valued? Is he or she too "big" for the firm already? What (if anything) will the new employee learn while working at this organization that will be of lasting value?

Today an individual joining an organization is as likely to approach that organization with skepticism as with excitement. With younger people, the mood is often, "I'll give the organization a try and see what it can do for me." Younger people coming into the workforce are far less intimidated than the group that came before them. They also are far less likely to make a commitment than their older peers.

Looking at organizations with skeptical eyes is good and bad. It's good because too few organizations have delivered on their promises. They have not become number one in their sector, a goal expressed in too many annual reports, and have not become innovation engines or learning organizations. Instead, they have merely gotten by. For every Intel or Home Depot or Apple or Coca Cola or IBM, there are dozens of companies characterized by high levels of mistrust, skepticism, and outright antipathy between most workers and the team at the top. Too many companies are in the grips of the problem I related pages ago, where the CEO mistrusts his or her subordinates and the subordinates mistrust the boss.

Looking at organizations skeptically is also bad in some respects. It is bad because organizations are weightless, mindless, and invisible. They are merely sets of rules and procedures by which we work together to accomplish goals we cannot accomplish on our own. In that case, if we look at organizations through skeptical eyes, then what we are doing is negating the effect we can have on the firm. We are invalidating ourselves as leaders by saying that the organization we are joining cannot be changed, that the packet of rules and the ways things are currently done cannot be changed by us. And yet what is an organization, and why should we regard it as sacrosanct?

To be a leader, we must view ourselves as capable of creating change. We must wake up each morning with the belief that the organization in which we work can be bent to the will of a group of thoughtful human beings and that the structure of the organization in which we work should not limit its purpose.

The goal of an organization is simply to accomplish a set of goals on a consistent basis. But we, not the organization, are the agents who do that. The organization is mute. We are the agents who hop on those flights and go to those meetings to make sure everyone is aligned around the same purpose. We are the ones who get things done.

LEADERS VERSUS MANAGERS

By now we all know that there is a difference between leading and managing—two important jobs that, according to the analysts, are very different. A great many observers have written about this fact. But I would take this observation a step further. In my view, we no longer need managers in the traditional sense—those who organize and execute on behalf of the leaders. What we need instead are leaders who can create a sense of common purpose so everyone executes and everyone leads. We need people who are well trained, embrace thought leadership, are positive, and are willing to work toward a common goal. We need *individuals,* in the best sense of the word, who can lead alongside a group of peers. We need people with a wide range of skills and with true mental agility. We need people who have internalized the values of the company—its brand, mission, and values—and can make decisions based on what they know. We need a new kind of leader who can get things done.

True, we still need to manage. We need people who can make the trains run on time, can make certain the deliveries arrive, and can take responsibility for systems and processes. But we don't need managers in the old-fashioned sense of people whose responsibility derives from someone else—people who must constantly seek permission before they can act.

What we need are people like the bellman at the Wynn Resorts who hopped into his car and drove from Las Vegas to Los Angeles to retrieve a guest's pills, entirely on his own initiative. What we need are more CEOs like FM Global's Shivan Subramaniam, who has the discipline to let others do jobs he enjoys, like poring over spreadsheets, so they will continue to grow and develop their sense of leadership and autonomy. We need to train people and work with people to achieve these ends.

These two examples—one from the so-called bottom rung of the corporation, a bellman, and one from the top, a CEO— should not be viewed as extremes. These two individuals are united in their respective organizations through the power of common purpose. They do what they need to do, go where they need to go (including taking red-eye flights), and help people in their organizations they need to help because they have disciplined and trained themselves to think from the point of view of *we,* and not just *me.* These two individuals are as different as any two people can be with regard to education, capabilities, skills, and point of view, but they are united in the sense that both act out of a sense of common purpose.

NEW LEADERS, NEW ORGANIZATION

Organizations are in flux, and so is leadership. Whether we like it or not, organizations will continue to become flatter, more technological, and more global. Individual careers will change, and people will change the way they work. In the age of Facebook, LinkedIn, Twitter, and who knows what is to come, it makes no sense to think that traditional organizational structures will continue to exist. Among knowledge workers especially, a number of different types of working relationships will be developing.

Organizations will come to resemble constellations of capabilities linked together technologically from centers located around the world. Some of these centers will be independent, some will be wholly owned, and some will have long-term alliances. And no matter what the politicians say, outsourcing will continue.

These indicators point to a future in which big companies will comprise smaller pieces, each with unique characteristics, ownership structures, and relationships. Each of these elements, when combined, will create enormous value.

What will keep it all together? Incentives can take us only part of the way. There are things more important than money, especially for younger workers. Mission, values, goals, and purpose count for a lot. And, of course, the chance to become part of a great team counts as well.

I believe that as organizations evolve, the power of common purpose will become the factor that differentiates winning organizations from those left behind. It will be the force leaders use to align the interests of people on their teams. Common purpose is a powerful force.

In the years ahead, leaders who can create common purpose will be in great demand. These leaders are likely to be kinder, more caring, and more empathic than leaders in the past. And by connecting with people on their teams at a human and purpose level, they are likely to create organizations superior to anything that has come before.

A LEADERSHIP LIBRARY

Over the years, I've read a lot of books about the art and practice of leadership. Many of them were little more than platitudes—interesting but not very useful and hardly transformative. The books listed here, however, offer thoughtful discussions about what it means to lead and the challenges leaders must overcome. Among the books on this list are some of my favorites—anything by Richard Boyatzis, for example, or Ronald Heifetz.

Some of the other books on the list are must reads because they make you think in new ways. That's why I list *The Power of Impossible Thinking: Transform the Business of Your Life and the Life of Your Business.* In addition, a few books offer simple, usable tools every leader needs to know how to use—for example, *Fierce Conversation: Achieving Success at Work and in Life, One Conversation at a Time.* I've used this book in my own work life and found it to have immense power.

Another book on the list is *Synchronicity: The Inner Path of Leadership,* by Joseph Jaworski and Betty Sue Flowers. This is an idiosyncratic, even odd, little book. I love it because it uncovers a simple truth: that leaders are individuals and each individual is unique. They think in their own ways, act in their own ways, and even view reality in their own ways. Before you disagree, think about it. If Steve Jobs or Bill Gates or Albert Einstein or Winston

Churchill saw reality just as everybody else did, the world would be a far different place.

Then there are the books by Warren Bennis, one of my and everyone else's mentors, and by Charles Handy, who could be called the Warren Bennis of Britain.

Have a look at these books, read them if you haven't already, and build your own leadership library. As you do, you'll come to understand the single most important idea about leadership: the more you know yourself and the more you understand others, the better you will lead.

The Art of the Long View: Planning for the Future in an Uncertain World, by Peter Schwartz. New York: Doubleday, 1991.

Beyond Race and Gender: Unleashing the Power of Your Total Work Force by Managing Diversity, by R. Roosevelt Thomas Jr. New York: Amacom, 1991.

The Corporate Culture Survival Guide, by Edgar H. Schein. San Francisco: Jossey-Bass, 1999.

Creating Value Through People, by Mercer Consulting. Hoboken, N.J.: Wiley, 2008.

The Essential Bennis, by Warren Bennis and Patricia Ward Biederman. San Francisco, Jossey-Bass, 2009.

Execution: The Discipline of Getting Things Done, by Larry Bossidy, Ram Charan, and Charles Burck. New York: Crown, 2002.

Fierce Conversations: Achieving Success at Work and in Life, One Conversation at a Time, by Susan Scott. New York: Viking, 2002.

Finding Flow: The Psychology of Engagement with Everyday Life, by Mihaly Csikszentmihalyi. New York: HarperCollins, 1990.

First, Break All the Rules: What the World's Greatest Managers Do Differently, by Marcus Buckingham and Curt Coffman. New York: Simon & Schuster, 1999.

Getting to Yes: Negotiating Agreement Without Giving In, by Bruce Patton, Roger Fisher, and William Ury. Boston: Houghton Mifflin, 1981, 1991.

Good to Great: Why Some Companies Make the Leap . . . and Others Don't, by Jim Collins. New York: HarperCollins, 2001.

The Handbook of Coaching: A Comprehensive Resource Guide for Managers, Executives, Consultants, and HR, by Frederic M. Hudson. San Francisco: Jossey-Bass, 1999.

The Heart of Change: Real-Life Stories of How People Change Their Organizations, by John P. Kotter and Dan S. Cohen. Boston: Harvard Business School Press, 2002.

The Leadership Challenge (4th ed.), by James M. Kouzes and Barry Z. Posner. San Francisco: Jossey-Bass, 2007.

Leadership Without Easy Answers, by Ronald Heifetz. Cambridge, Mass.: Harvard University Press, 1998.

Managing Transitions: Making the Most of Change, by William Bridges. Cambridge, Mass.: Da Capo Press, 1991, 2003.

MBA in a Book: Mastering Business with Attitude, by Joel Kurtzman, Glenn Rifkin, and Victoria Griffith. New York: Crown, 2008.

Myself, by Charles Handy. New York: Amacom, 2006, 2008.

On Becoming a Leader, by Warren Bennis. Philadelphia: Perseus Books Group, 1989, 2004.

The Power of Impossible Thinking: Transform the Business of Your Life and the Life of Your Business, by Jerry Wind, Colin Crook, and Robert Gunther. Philadelphia: Wharton School Publishing, 2006.

The Power of Purpose: Creating Meaning in Your Life and Work, by Richard J. Leider. San Francisco: Berrett-Koehler, 1997, 2004.

Presence: Human Purpose and the Field of the Future, by Peter M. Senge, C. Otto Scharmer, Joseph Jaworski, and Betty Sue Flowers. New York: Doubleday, 2004.

Primal Leadership: Learning to Lead with Emotional Intelligence, by Daniel Goleman, Richard Boyatzis, and Anne McKee. Boston: Harvard Business School Press, 2002.

Resonant Leadership: Renewing Yourself and Connecting with Others Through Mindfulness, Hope, and Compassion, by Richard E. Boyatzis and Annie McKee. Boston: Harvard Business School Press, 2005.

Synchronicity: The Inner Path of Leadership, by Joseph Jaworski and Betty Sue Flowers. San Francisco: Berrett-Koehler, 1996, 1998.

What Got You Here Won't Get You There: How Successful People Become Even More Successful, by Marshall Goldsmith and Mark Reiter. New York, New York: Hyperion, 2007.

ABOUT THE AUTHOR

Joel Kurtzman is chairman of the Kurtzman Group, a research and consulting firm focusing on issues relating to knowledge management, strategy, economic development, global risk, governance, and thought leadership. He is a senior fellow at the Milken Institute and publisher of *The Milken Institute Review*; a member of the editorial board of MIT's *Sloan Management Review*; and a senior fellow at Wharton's SEI Center. He is an advisor to the World Economic Forum and to the US Council on Competitiveness. Previously, he was the editor of the Harvard Business Review, founder and editor of *strategy+business* magazine, a columnist at *Fortune*, and an editor and columnist at *The New York Times*.

For more than thirty years, Kurtzman has interviewed, worked with, and consulted to the CEOs of some of the world's largest companies. He has consulted to Microsoft; Mercer Management; Littler Mendelson; Booz, Allen & Hamilton; Korn/Ferry International; Aramark; Clayton Dubilier & Rice; AEA Investments; Heidrick & Struggles; Dow Jones; and the governments of Italy and Spain. As the global lead partner for Thought Leadership and Innovation at PricewaterhouseCoopers, Kurtzman was responsible for developing new, marketable ideas in strategy, technology, the capital markets, and business policy.

Kurtzman was an international economist at the United Nations and responsible for nineteen teams of researchers in 23 countries engaged in large-scale, global economic forecasting and policy-making programs. He co-led the UN's research into the "new international economic order," which focused on the world's economic transition to a more market-based structure. While at the UN, Kurtzman was involved as a negotiator between India and the Union Carbide Corporation over the Bhopal disaster. In 2000, he was awarded India's Indira Gandhi Prize from the Priyadarshni Academy in Mumbai.

Kurtzman has lectured around the world, testified before the U.S. House of Representatives, hosted television and radio programs on business and economics, and served as chairman and speaker at numerous conferences. He has spoken and moderated panels on corporate governance and other issues at Davos and at many European, Asian, and Latin American forums, and at Microsoft's CEO Summit. Kurtzman was the on-air business book reviewer on CNN.

Kurtzman is the author of twenty-one books on business and economics, as well as hundreds of articles. Kurtzman earned his AB at the University of California, Berkeley, where he was the recipient of the Eisner Memorial Award, the highest award given to a student by the university. He earned his master's at the University of Houston and was the recipient of a Moody Foundation Fellowship. He has served on public and private company boards and on the boards of nonprofit organizations.

For more information, please visit www.kurtzmangroup.com.

INDEX